MY ONE TRUE LOVE

EDITED BY CARO LLEWELLYN

RANDOM HOUSE AUSTRALIA

Also by Caro Llewellyn and available from Random House:

Fresh! Market People and their Food

The Tartan Jigsaw Puzzle (appeared in *Women Love Sex*)

Jobs for the Girls (co-authored with Skye Rogers)

For Peter
My once-in-a-lifetime

Published by
Random House Australia Pty Ltd
20 Alfred Street, Milsons Point, NSW 2061
http://www.randomhouse.com.au

Sydney New York Toronto
London Auckland Johannesburg
and agencies throughout the world

First published 1999
Copyright © Caro Llewellyn 1999

All rights reserved. No part of this publication may be reproduced, stored in a retrieval system, or transmitted in any form or by any means, electronic, mechanical, photocopying, recording or otherwise, without the prior written permission of the Publisher.

National Library of Australia
Cataloguing-in-Publication Data

My one true love: twenty-one writers on love passion and obsession

ISBN 0 091 83704 9.

1. Love-Miscellanea. 2. Authors – Miscellanea. I.
2. Llewellyn, Caro, 1965–

152.41

Poetry reproduced with the kind permission of Peter Woods
Typeset by Asset Typesetting Pty Ltd, Sydney
Printed by Griffin Press Pty Ltd

10 9 8 7 6 5 4 3 2 1

Acknowledgements

My sincere thanks to Margaret Sullivan who so enthusiastically embraced the theme and possibility of this anthology. I told Margaret about wanting to edit a book called *My One True Love* over dinner in a Melbourne restaurant. Strangely, because titles are often the last thing to come to mind for a book, this name came to me first and the idea for a book flowed from that. Margaret was immediately positive and we spent the rest of the night using the paper tablecloth as a notebook. She drew a huge love heart, the size of the table and we brainstormed names of people to approach, writing them in the heart. The list, tentative at first, grew and grew as our meal progressed and when I sat down to start this project, I opened up the oil-stained tablecloth, now crumpled and began letters to all those in our big heart.

When Margaret Sullivan left Random House to go overseas, I was worried for *My One True Love*, but I needn't have been. Jody Lee worked as if *My One True Love* had been hers from the beginning. Her sensitive editing and dedication to every detail has strengthened this book immeasurably. Always positive and cheerful—it has been an enriching collaboration.

Thanks to Fiona Inglis, my agent, and giver of sage advice and direction.

Special thanks to Jenny Evans without whose help I would have struggled. Jenny typed the stories that weren't on disk for me—a laborious and tiresome task that she did swiftly, cheerfully and accurately.

Heartfelt gratitude to Becky Llewellyn for her advice, encouragement, feedback and kind reading.

This book would not have been possible, of course, without the insight, honesty and understanding of those whose pieces and stories you will read. Thank you to all those who divulged their passions, wrote stories and took time to consider the idea of true love.

Thank you to those who wrote stories but are not included here. It was a very difficult task indeed to choose some works above others and I thank you and am sorry that space and time did not permit me to use all the pieces I was sent.

In memory of Don Dunstan

Contents

Introduction	1
Dorothy Porter	9
Margaret Scott	13
Philip Cox	27
Garry Disher	35
Rosie Scott	45
Meme McDonald	53
Don Dunstan	63
Nicholas Jose	77
Emma Tom	85
Adib Khan	103
Elizabeth Jolley	115
Gretel Killeen	121
José Borghino	139
Robert Drewe	149
Mike Coward	159
Barry Divola	167

Amy Witting	177
Nikki Gemmell	201
Raimondo Cortese	211
Robert Dessaix	227
Paul Cox	235
Author Biographies	240

INTRODUCTION

Listening to the radio one morning, I was forced to consider the meaning of true love. A Northern Territory woman was being interviewed about how she assisted her husband to die. He was terminally ill and in pain, and she helped him to end his life. Her adoration of him was so great that in his interest she could let him go, help him to leave her forever. The emotional complexity of her act floored me: the pain and suffering borne from aiding the death of someone close, the public outcry at her actions, her loss and her love. I wondered if I could do something so compassionate and selfless.

When do we really consider what we cherish? Not simply to list all that is dear to our heart in an abstract way, but to actually imagine the richness we would lose if the one thing that gives meaning to our world was suddenly gone.

When, for example, do we fully realise the profound bond we have with our children? I worry if my son is sick or is away for any length of time. If he is threatened or unhappy then I am achingly aware of the depth of my feelings for him, but the rest of the time, he and I float in a daily routine that skims the surface of our true emotions. Of course as parents, it would be too painful, and counterproductive and we would never let go or grow, if we constantly envisaged life without our children, but to sit occasionally and ponder our feelings about those we love is something I think we do too little.

It's not that I don't think of my child in a loving way every day, or regularly say the words 'I love you Jack-a-lack', but the affection or attention I show if I actually picture my life without him is of an entirely different order. With that thought in mind, I will happily lie down beside him when he can't get to sleep, even if my dinner is getting cold on the table and I am weak with hunger; I will pack up my work and go to the park for a game of football, no matter how important the job; I will pull myself out of the warm and caressing arms of slumber to hear all about Ninjas and Game

My One True Love

Boys and who's who in the schoolyard hierarchy, when my body aches for sleep. When I realise that he will eventually leave to build a life of his own, I take nothing for granted and I enjoy every moment of him. My voice softens, I pay more attention and I take better care. In short, I become a better mother.

Loves signpost our lives. We can map our past by that which has been special to our hearts: by the people we have loved, by certain places, laden with memory and meaning, and by the ideals that have motivated our life choices. Many of our loves change with time. They ebb and flow and are redefined by new experiences and change as inevitably as the sea turns. Loves are discarded, or fade to insignificance when something more arresting comes along. Some we grow out of, others we are betrayed by.

Sometimes when we look back at past loves, we ask ourselves what moved us so deeply at the time? Time wears away the significance, making it hard in the face of new passions, to imagine that the object of our attention could have had such an impact.

In the course of our lives many things will grab our hearts' attention, but I believe we reach some peace, some state of grace, when we discover or acknowledge our one true love. Not like others, that one true love is a passion—a deep and true emotion that changes with time but never fades. Our one true love informs, motivates and guides us: it is a spark that makes life worth living. Philip Cox's passion is as exciting to him today as it was when he first encountered it. Challenging, changing and always interesting. It is deep and profound. His love is nourishing and yet in need of his attention. It is a love that gives as equally as it demands and remains, after all these years, the object of his desire and curiosity.

I wanted to discover the one thing that people could not live happily without. Going public about this was not a prospect everyone wanted to consider. Australian culture does not lend itself easily to honest and open declarations. We are not comfortable with showing our hand, opening our hearts in exuberance. We applaud the understatement, enjoy averting the gaze of others and often hide our true selves behind masks and charades. I was not surprised, then, when some people declined to submit. Many were busy with other projects and commitments, but in some cases, the letters I received stating reasons for not adding their voice to this collection gave me insight into just how confronting a task I had set. One man wrote that after

INTRODUCTION

consulting with his wife, he had to admit that his passion for life was work. This, he said, was not something he wanted to share with the world. Another person I approached wondered how they could remain true to the declarations they gave their partner after writing a story with film in the leading role. To write without offending is not an easy task.

To arrive at our one true love with open arms and a warm embrace, around which nothing else matters, we have to make a list in our minds of all that brings us joy. Isolating that one thing that makes life meaningful and joyous is difficult. If I were to choose between my partner and my son, I would necessarily be discounting someone truly dear to me. My life without either of them would be a shell and I would not like to choose.

Obviously, while they are in an altogether different league, there are other loves that I rate highly, without which I think my life would not be worth much. I would not like to consider a world without books, for example. To imagine never being transported to another world with the turn of a page, or being able to see the lives of others described in text, or to have my views challenged by a book is indeed a desolate prospect.

I cannot envisage an existence without the sea or my closest friends. I would sorely miss spaghetti if it were never again to be twirled on my fork, but I would not miss pasta in any of its other forms, like linguini or penne which pale in comparison. Olive oil is essential to my life. That rich dark green (it has to be extra virgin) liquid brings me such joy. I believe that olives are sacred.

The truth is of course, though, that there are many loves that I could actually go on living without. If I had to. Some, however, I could not. I am a coward who has set a task for others that I am not willing to undertake myself. How does one nominate an ultimate, when our lives are full of many: family, children, lovers, careers, hobbies, place, ideas, beliefs?

My brief to contributors was very broad. Their stories could be fictional or true and Dorothy Porter submitted a poem. The only stipulation I made was that the theme involve an essential love. No wonder, then, that this collection is vast in its embrace. From Emma Tom's character who has trouble distinguishing past and present loves and bundles them under the name Ray, to Robert Drewe's disturbing story of a murderer, we are offered a broad definition of the meaning of love. At first, some of the stories I received didn't seem to fit the brief, but when I considered them more closely, I realised my idea of an essential love had been too narrow, not that the writers had stretched the boundaries.

Raimondo Cortese's contribution spotlights the stage and his desire to make great art, yet it goes beyond describing his passion, explaining his hopes and fears for the form. His objective is to explain, protect and expand his life's focus.

The object of our love reflects what we honour and believe in. It signifies the ideals and hopes we have for our lives. Don Dunstan's relishing of the simple task of cooking and providing beautiful food for his friends and family brought him spiritual and emotional joy every day. Don's story not only informs us about food—his discovery of it, the way it brings people together, the ceremony and history of cooking, but most significantly, it teaches us something about who he really was.

When I first considered this anthology, I felt Australia had come to a troubled point in its history. A new political party, One Nation, was driving a wedge through the heart of Australian goodwill and honour. *Bringing Them Home, The Report of the National Inquiry into the Separation of Aboriginal and Torres Strait Islander Children from Their Families* was tabled in the Federal Parliament, prompting tears from many and the refusal of an apology from the Prime Minister. When John Howard refused to say sorry to Aboriginal Australia, I knew we were in serious trouble. For the first time in my life, I felt deeply ashamed to be Australian.

Needless to say, I was thrilled to receive Meme McDonald's *The Vine*, a story of forbidden love. The joy between two children—one black, one white—is stamped out with terror and shame. Meme interweaves issues—society's taboos, the power we have to constrict the lives of others and what it is to live with a secret in your heart. On a bigger canvas, though, we could read this as an allegory; a nation is forced to confront its past and slowly, slowly, with the help of those it has betrayed, learns to forgive itself.

Where *The Vine* searches for closure and understanding, Nikki Gemmell's *My Name is Disturbance* self-consciously avoids reconciliation. In this story, Nikki's character walks away from her beloved, into the arms of another. *My Name is Disturbance* is a meditation on choice and the commitment one must make to art; a dedication that sometimes looks

INTRODUCTION

selfish and without reason, and as it turns out, can never really be understood or explained.

The painter John Olsen in his memoir *Drawn from Life* makes the comment that Australia's vast landscape can only be seen in its true form from the air. *Up Above the World* by Garry Disher shows just how evasive this land can be, even from an aerial perspective. Having flown above it with his brother hundreds of times, having mapped and detailed it for the war against the Japanese, the protagonist in this story discovers the landscape has tricked him: he realises that he doesn't understand it. This piece about our place in the Australian landscape is overlaid with the story of two brothers and the sad realisation that the soul mate our young cartographer thought he had never really existed.

Landscapes we knew as children remain deeply ingrained in our memories and I expected in advance that a number of the contributions would focus on place and the impact our surroundings have on us. Nicholas Jose and Rosie Scott describe beautiful places, but both authors have added meaning and dimension to the landscape, writing about childhood, longing and loss in a broader sense.

Of course in an anthology about love, one would expect disappointment. How could there not be, since love is capable of great pain? Margaret Scott's character is crushed when she realises the wonderful interior world she has built for herself and her doll could be smashed up in a moment. From the eyes of a raggedy old doll and her puppeteer, we peer out through the great backyard jungle and remember how unintentionally brutal adults can be to the fantastical world of children.

It is interesting to see so many contributors looked to their early childhood. Then, it seemed, true love was in our hearts because we were not tainted with cynicism, we were carefree and open to possibilities. *Baba: My Song ... Widows and Nephews and all ...* is almost a love letter, or better put, a letter of love, from Elizabeth Jolley to her sister, Baba. She remembers sharing measles, cutting tufts out of her hair, calming her to sleep and always, always being there for her little Baba.

The painful years of adolescence—a time when our very rite of passage seems to be bound up tightly with heartbreak and frustrated emotions—had to feature in a collection with this theme. Barry Divola's *Sissy Bar* looks with crystalline clarity and attention to every detail of time and space, at the agony of unrequited crushes. It's interesting how we are often able to remember what we were doing when we were dumped, more clearly than we can recall some of the highs of togetherness. That focus says a lot about our hearts and why we grow to shield them.

As a counterpoint, though, José Borghino's *Monsieur Poltarac Eats Cheese* is a call to action. José reminds us of the dangers of hiding our intentions behind too many veils. We want to whisper in the ears of Monsieur Poltarac and the beautiful widowed Mirabelle, to stop being so silly, but they can not hear us and we must watch as they tragically slip away from each other.

Too often love is thought of as only a playmate for the young. We throw all our congratulations on the youthful and the beautiful and reflect those romantic images in the media. I am pleased that this collection lifts the covers and shows some ageing bodies between the sheets as well. We live in a throwaway age and sometimes we forget that it takes work and commitment to keep something precious. We watch movie stars and supermodels marry in a whirlwind, fairy princess, white wedding dream only to read their real-life 'I married a maniac', everything revealed world exclusive, two months later. Sometimes we need to be reminded that love can last a lifetime and also that it is not just for the trim and tanned.

True love is not always the bearer of happy tidings. Nor do we always behave well in its gaze. Robert Dessaix's fiction looks at a love built on flickering glimpses. Despite its lack of reality and substance, this is a love with long tendrils, that continues to haunt and embrace well into old age and causes some shockingly wonderful bad behaviour.

Gretel Killeen also paints a not so picture perfect unison. Describing the consuming, glorious, confusing and disarming desire of a younger man and an older woman, she then shows us its dark side. These two weave a web from which neither can escape. Obsession, jealousy and violence, in the end, are not enough to stop this dance, this headiness they both long to drink, fully aware of its poison. Gretel asks us each to question what role we play in dangerous dances.

Each true love is unique. Whether it be an object, a place, a ritual, a person or an idea, we will bring to it our own meaning and significance. I thought a collection of writings that prompted us to consider that which is most important to us would be an antidote to some of the negativity in

INTRODUCTION

today's society. In considering what we love, hate, anger and hurt fall away. Thinking about what we cherish makes other quests less meaningful. If we contemplate losing or becoming estranged from that one thing we hold dearest to our heart, then we realise the futility of endeavours that fill and cloud our lives.

As film-maker Paul Cox so aptly puts it, with our one true love in mind, we can find our true spirit, 'everything becomes more humane, more alive.'

DOROTHY PORTER

Europa

EUROPA

*No wonder you love
Europa*

*You will never crack
the crust
of this blinding ice moon
and dredge its slush.*

*If its thin cold air
could ever fizz
in brave human lungs
you would still be the last
to breathe it.*

*You're happy
for Europa
to stay in its remote orbit
showering down
the odd twinkling tick
to squat in your skin.*

*So much easier
to scratch its itch
and laze
   in enigma*

*than love
   and render to
the drunk woman
   in blinding distress
dirtying your street.*

MARGARET SCOTT

Lizzie and the Great Outdoors

*T*he back garden was very small and bounded on three sides by high walls topped by little wooden fences. Along the narrow fence tops cats would suddenly come stalking, small tigers in the sky, remote and alien as clouds or shadows passing smoothly behind glass. Lizzie watched them sometimes when she was playing in the corner by the coal-house wall—but would no more have thought of trying to waylay one of these passersby than of reaching up to halt the stars in their courses.

Her world was in the earth, especially the big shady bed of dark loam where the French beans swarmed upwards over a rampart of tall sticks, embellishing the air with green curlicues and scarlet flowers. Along the front of the bed was a row of heavy stones leaning uphill to divide the banked soil from the lawn. And here between two stones Mowgli had his house. The roof was made of a little piece of polished wood that might have been sawn from an architrave. It was a dark mottled chestnut colour, curved and very smooth. Under this lid Mowgli could sleep contentedly on a bed of grass clippings among his spears and stores of berries with a tiny saucepan, brought from the dolls' house, nestling among his neatly piled firewood.

Mowgli was made of felt, thin, pliant, and orangey-brown. He had begun as a six-inch fairy doll with flaxen hair, gauze skirt and wand. Stripped little by little of every ornament except his white underpants he had changed his sex and embarked on a new life in the great outdoors. In

Lizzie's hand or suspended from a bit of cotton he bounced across the lawn, scaled the buddleia, hunted beetles, woodlice and ants, and gathered fragments of petal and leaf for his salads. Yet he was much more than a puppet. The big staring dolls who sat in a schoolroom row at the top of the house, waiting to be smacked and ordered about on rainy days, offered puny little Lizzie the pleasure of absolute power over their existence. Mowgli did something different. He was the agent of creation through whom the meticulously tended little garden became a wild exotic world of great plains, trees with spikes of purple bloom as long and thick as a man's body, and strange groves hung with shining scarlet fruit bigger than giant pumpkins. There were structures here more gigantic, more mysterious than the pyramids, more wonderful than anything in the ruined city of the *Jungle Book*: cliffs of enormous bricks; a pair of terracotta urns spilling leaves the size of tea-trays and blossoms as big as human heads; highways of room-sized slabs of smooth stone, and a vast cavern, like a cathedral, filled with slopes of glossy black boulders rising into the distant cobwebby darkness.

As well as all this, Mowgli was the means by which Lizzie herself was created anew, not just because she controlled his every action but because together they performed amazing, death-defying physical feats. Lizzie, in the ordinary way, was a bony little thing, always ailing, and, although she passionately longed to be a boy, was hopeless at climbing trees or catching balls. But Mowgli could leap from a standing position to halfway up the buddleia tree and then, without even a swinging vine to help him, cross in one great agile bound to the French beans. He was never tired, never ill and, when he fell from some enormous height, never harmed. If he got wet on a night of rain, when snails crawled into his house and stuck themselves to his ceiling, he could be dried out in the morning. If he got muddy he could be washed and if his arm got torn, as it once did when he was prising thorns for arrowheads off a rose bush, he simply went into a trance until he had been sewn together with neat orange stitches.

The only real danger that Lizzie and Mowgli faced came in the form of invading giants who sometimes clumped down the steps from the cement ramp by the garage, round the circular bed and on to their grass. Lizzie's mother occasionally set about digging daisies out of the lawn with a special fork or carted a deckchair down from the garage to sit and sew in the sun. But she, though sometimes puzzled and anxious, was the least intrusive of the invaders. It was quite possible for Mowgli to flit to some point out of her line of vision and for Lizzie to hunch herself up in a small cone of concentration where, so long as she remembered not to speak aloud, she was quite safe. The story of Mowgli's adventurous afternoon could spin on in silence, his actions matching the words that ran through Lizzie's head:

'One day Mowgli decided to go out to the Great Prickle Tree beyond the Big Rocks to collect some spiky needles for knitting a cloak and for skewers in his meat. He took some apples for his dinner wrapped up in a cloth tied to his belt. He took a big stick and set out without a care in the world. He climbed the rocks beside his house and made his way along the Big Brown Plain to the place where he could jump down to the lovely soft grass by the Prickle Tree. He knew he must be very careful because the prickles were deadly poison ... no—the prickles were very sharp. "Ha! Ha!" he said. "I should have brought my sack ..."'

'What's that, dear?'

'Nothing,' said Lizzie crossly. 'I didn't say anything.'

'You said something about a sack.'

Lizzie kept quite still, biting her lip and viciously nipping spines from the little conifer that, every year, was dug up, put in a pot and hung with fairylights.

'Was it part of your game?'

'I was just making up a story about a Christmas tree.'

'Oh! Father Christmas's sack!'

Lizzie didn't bother to reply. She stared at Mowgli, fidgeting him backwards and forwards until the stupid clumsy pretence of Father Christmas had sunk away and the delicate magic of the prickle hunt had restored itself.

'"I wonder if these soft green needles are good to eat," he said. "Mmm! They're sweet as sugarcane. I'll make a bundle and tie it with my string. I always carry string in my dinner-bag and my pink knife I made from a piece of shell. These other stiff old needles will make good skewers. I wonder if I could find some really long ones to make arrows for my bow!" And with this Mowgli whipped out his trusty knife and began to cut lots of big needles from the Great Prickle Tree.'

Lizzie's mother sighed. She was glad in a way that Lizzie was so well behaved, never wanting to run off and play in the street, but she worried over the way she kept to herself all the time. It must come, she thought, from being so delicate and having to spend all those weeks shut away in a sickroom when she was tiny.

But Lizzie's father was less easygoing. He complained about flowers nipped from his tomato plants and he didn't like Mowgli's house being where it was. He thought it looked untidy—that bit of wood stuck in his neat row of stones. People must wonder, he said to Lizzie's mother, when they came to look at his beans. When he got up on the bed to attend to his framework of sticks he carefully avoided looking at this feet as though, it seemed to Lizzie, he wouldn't have been sorry if, apparently by mistake, he'd stepped back on Mowgli's house and crushed it.

One day Mr Cheshire from next door was invited to inspect the crop. Mr Cheshire was a natty widower in his early forties with patent leather hair and a flat moustache. He had a housekeeper who cooked his meals and cleaned his house, a car and a good job at Filton aeroplane works. Lizzie's mother had an idea that he'd fallen in love with her younger sister, Virgie, so whenever Virgie came to supper, Lizzie's mother got out the Crown Derby dinner service, cooked something special, and asked Mr Cheshire to call around at about seven.

'He's a good catch,' she told her sister as they bustled about together getting the meal.

Virgie, who wore perky hats, high heels and very red lipstick, tossed her head. She was still getting letters from an American lieutenant she'd met at a dance.

'He's not as good-looking as Artie,' she said, but when Mr Cheshire came out into the kitchen on his way to look over the beans, she turned the colour of the tomatoes she'd sliced to arrange on the salad in its cut-glass bowl.

Out in the garden Mr Cheshire caught sight of Mowgli's roof, picked it up and waggled it about in a rallying sort of way.

'Been doing a bit of woodwork, Ted?'

This, for Lizzie's father, was the last straw. He scooped up Mowgli and the saucepan, dropped them on the coal-house windowsill and brushed away all Mowgli's household supplies with his fingertips.

'Some mess of Lizzie's,' he said and shied the roof into the kindling box just inside the coal-house door.

When Lizzie went out into the garden after school next day, she couldn't believe her eyes. At first she thought of throwing herself on the grass and screaming until she made herself ill. She pictured her mother running out, her father carrying her up to bed, her own face all hot and teary against her pillow, and Dr Merchant sitting on the bed, taking her pulse.

'Daddy broke my house,' she'd tell them, still sobbing. And her mother and the doctor would turn and stare accusingly at her father. But the more she thought of all this, the more frightened she became at the prospect of such an enormous upset. When she pictured her mother's rage against her father she began to feel quite sorry for him.

'I ask you,' her mother would say, 'I ask you what harm was the child doing? Don't try to get round me with your excuses. It's self, self, self with you, Ted, and I'm sick, weary and tired of it …'

So Lizzie started making a new house for Mowgli in the rockery. She dug out a neat rectangle in the slope near one of the rocks and lined the inside walls with small stones pressed into the earth. The front of the house was left open so that Mowgli could get a view of his whole kingdom. When Lizzie rescued his roof from the kindling box and put it in place it was clear that the new dwelling was far finer as well as safer than the old one. Since it was nearly suppertime Mowgli had to get his bedding together very quickly. Tomorrow would be a busy day with fresh supplies of food and fuel to be gathered …

Meanwhile, pausing over his tripe and onions, Lizzie's father said, 'So when are we going to hear those wedding bells?'

'You can laugh,' said Lizzie's mother, 'but he'll ask her sure as eggs, believe you me.'

Virgie began coming round for supper more often than before. Lizzie didn't like her much even though it was she who had given Lizzie the fairy doll from whom Mowgli had emerged like a butterfly from a lifeless-looking chrysalis. Virgie was mad about clothes and hair, always criticising the way Lizzie looked, always jerking at her hems and tweaking at her sleeves.

'Oh Peg! You can't let her go about in that old thing! Why don't you put a bit of a curl in her hair? It's like a yard of pump water! Why don't you get her something with a nice puffed sleeve? …'

Fortunately Virgie was too busy nowadays to bother much with Lizzie anymore. She spent all her time talking to Lizzie's mother about the two men in her life and, when she and Peg were settled side by side in the back garden, she forgot completely that Lizzie was even there. But Lizzie, entranced for the first time by what Auntie Virgie had to say to her mother, often found tasks for Mowgli that took her close up behind the two deckchairs. While Mowgli gathered grass for his bed or tore up daisy leaves, Lizzie would squat in the chairs' shadow, quiet as a mouse, willing Auntie Virgie to stay true to handsome Artie Schwartz. It was as though Virgie had two separate existences like a film star—one in the everyday world where she went on being her ordinary bossy self, the other up in the silvery realm of romance where she became the heroine you longed to see living happily ever after with a hero far more dashing than Mr Cheshire.

Sometimes the duel being played out between Virgie's two lovers became so intense Mowgli dropped from Lizzie's hand and, overcome by unaccustomed lethargy, fell asleep, unheeded, in the shade of Virgie's deckchair.

'Of course, Artie's very romantic. Everyone says he's the image of Alan Ladd.'

'You can't live on romance, Virg. You've got to think. You don't even know if he's got a job to go back to.'

'He used to run this drugstore. I told you. In this little town in Oregon.'

'Drugstore? What, a chemist's like Boots or something? Does he own the shop himself?'

'I think so. He's not short of money, Peg.'

'But you don't know what this drugstore place amounts to. It could be just some one-eyed little shop. You could get out there and find yourself dishing out syrup of figs until you drop.'

'Oh, I don't think Artie would ever let me work.'

'They can say anything they like while they're over here. Make out they'll give you the world when all the time they haven't got tuppence. But you know where you are with Mr Cheshire. You'd have that car and everything. And he'll always have that job according to Ted. It's not just for the duration like a lot of them in munitions …'

'But Artie's so generous!'

'Generous now he's got money to throw about. What about when the war's over and you're out there in this Oregon and it turns out he hasn't got the price of a hot meal? What about that?'

Despite all Artie's virtues, Virgie started going about with Mr Cheshire in his car. They went to the pictures to see *Gone with the Wind*, after which Virgie admitted that Mr Cheshire looked a bit like Clark Gable. She went next door to admire his golfing trophies, was shown over the house and introduced to the Welsh housekeeper, Mrs Evans, who served up tea and rock-cakes in the dining-room.

'You drink that while it's hot,' said Mrs Evans to Mr Cheshire.

'I will, I will. Don't I always do as I'm told like a good boy?'

Mr Cheshire thought this was a great joke and winked at Virgie but afterwards Virgie told Lizzie's mother that Mrs Evans was an old dragon.

'If I ever did—you know—I wouldn't keep her on for five minutes.'

'Well, he wouldn't expect to have a housekeeper once he was married again.'

'Oh, I'd want someone. With him bringing in all that money I'm not getting down on my knees scrubbing floors. But I couldn't put up with her. Nasty old biddy, bossing him about. Her and her cats. They're the ones that get up on your fence, you know. I'd complain about it if I were you.'

Even after things had advanced to this stage Virgie still went on at times about Artie. She couldn't resist the pleasure of pirouetting for just a little longer high on the peak of her eternal triangle. This was her way of enjoying a last fling before she settled down to married life. And she didn't want anyone to run away with the idea that Bill Cheshire could have her just for the asking, although she hadn't actually told Bill himself that he had a rival. Being so much older, Bill was inclined to be jealous and was always saying how disgusting it was to see British girls making themselves cheap with the Yanks. So Virgie had to make do with teasing her sister and her girlfriends in the typing-pool where she worked.

'It's really Artie I love,' she'd sigh. 'In my heart he's still king.' But after a while nobody except Lizzie believed her.

In July, about a month before V.J. Day, something terrible happened. One Saturday afternoon Virgie got up from her deckchair so quickly that Lizzie barely had time to scuttle back a few yards before her aunt turned round and saw her. Mowgli was left lying on the lawn. Virgie caught sight of him, snatched him up and went pink with indignation.

'This is that lovely little doll I gave you for Christmas! Look, Peg, what she's done! Pulled off all the little clothes and all the hair and everything! Destructive little monkey!'

'She still plays with it though, Virg. It's her favourite, isn't it, dear?'

'Well, I'spose I could fix it. Not that she deserves it, mind you.'

And to Lizzie's horror Virgie opened her big shiny handbag, tossed Mowgli down among the lipsticks and hair-pins and snapped the bag shut.

'You don't need to bother,' said Lizzie's mother. 'She likes it as it is.'

'Nobody could like it like that. What, is she daft or something?'

Lizzie crept to her mother, gripped her arm and looked up imploringly at her face. But Peg only smiled weakly and tried to avoid Lizzie's eye. She wanted her daughter to be a nice normal little girl. She wasn't going to do anything more to convince Virgie that Lizzie had an unnatural taste in dolls.

Lizzie felt quite sick. She thought again of starting a screaming fit but saw at once, where everyone would understand her being upset over a broken toy, nobody was going to understand why she didn't want one mended. There was nothing to be done. She had to watch Mowgli carted away in his swinging prison to be twisted and turned in Virgie's fingers with their long red nails, stabbed with needles and changed back into a namby-pamby thing that couldn't throw a spear to save its life.

She had one last quick glimpse of Mowgli before he was taken away to Auntie Virgie's house. When the deckchairs had been stowed away, Virgie took out an envelope of photographs that Artie had sent her from Berlin. She giggled in an 'aren't I awful' kind of way as she spread them out on the table for Peg to see.

'Just look at that profile, will you!'

She gazed at it with her head on one side.

'You ought to write,' said Lizzie's mother shortly.

'Oh yes, well, all in good time.'

Still giggling Virgie packed up the photos and pushed them back into her bag. Lizzie, leaning close, spotted Mowgli's orange leg, sticking up from under Artie's envelope.

The transformation happened very quickly. Three days later Mowgli came back, totally restored as Fairy Twinkletoes and wrapped in white tissue paper. Virgie unveiled him proudly on the kitchen table.

'Look!' she said. 'I even put a little star on the wand!'

Lizzie thanked her in a dull voice and took Mowgli upstairs. She was determined to rescue him from all his feminine encumbrances as soon as she could, but when she looked at him closely she saw that Virgie had done a much better job than the commercial maker who'd put the fairy doll together in the first place. This time Mowgli's white bodice was sewn to his skin around the neck and arm-holes and his blond hair, instead of being stuck on with a dab of glue, was embroidered into his scalp. It was going to be very difficult to cut him loose without mangling him in the process. Worst of all, he seemed to accept his renovation quite placidly as though he was really glad to be a fairy again and his wild, free spirit had fled away forever.

Lizzie moped for days, refusing to play in the garden and looking so forlorn that when she finally asked her mother to make her a new Mowgli doll, Peg gave in at once.

'Just don't let Auntie Virgie see it,' she said. 'We don't want to hurt her feelings.'

The felt they bought was a better colour than Old Mowgli's skin—tan rather than orange—and Lizzie's mother went to a lot of trouble in giving New Mowgli a fine head of short black curls made with French knots.

'You could call him Little Sambo,' she said.

But Lizzie pretended not to hear this. She took New Mowgli off to introduce him to his territory and had a wonderful time getting to know his strengths and weaknesses as he went about exploring plain and jungle. He had more stuffing than Old Mowgli, who'd been almost totally flat, so that he had trouble squeezing between rocks. On the other hand, if his feet were properly wedged, his stiffness made it easy for him to stand without flopping over. After going right round the garden together, Lizzie and New Mowgli called in at the home in the rockery, then bounded off past the mint bed to inspect the coal-house. But here New Mowgli's tour ended abruptly.

To Lizzie's great astonishment she found that Lucky, one of Mrs Evans's cats from next door, had come down from the fence top, settled herself in the kindling box and produced a litter of squirming black kittens.

Lizzie ran at once to tell her mother and Mrs Evans who came hurrying round with a basket lined with flannel to take the kittens home to Mr Cheshire's house. Lizzie knelt beside the old woman, peeping sideways at the crinkles in her neck and helping to lift the kittens out of the box.

'Auntie Virgie doesn't like cats,' said Lizzie.

Mrs Evans looked put out.

'Is that right? Well, I daresay she'll come round. Everyone likes my Lucky when they get to know her.'

Lizzie pondered this for a few moments.

'But Auntie Virgie won't get to know her. She isn't going to marry Mr Cheshire.'

'Is that right?' said Mrs Evans again, turning to stare at Lizzie. 'I heard it was just about settled.'

'Oh no. She loves Artie. In her heart he's still king.'

'Artie? Who's that?'

'Artie's an American soldier. He runs a drugstore in a place called Oregon. He's not there now though, because he's been in the war. He's in Berlin. The other day he sent Auntie Virgie all these photos of him and his friends standing in the bomb damage.'

Mrs Evans seemed tickled to death by this news. She pinched Lizzie's cheek and told her she must come next door to play with the kittens when they had their eyes open. Then she put Lucky under one arm and the basket under the other and went off home even more quickly than she'd arrived.

That evening there was a dreadful uproar in the kitchen.

'You must've let something slip,' Virgie shouted at Peg.

'I never did! How can you think such a thing?'

Virgie slumped on to a chair and hid her face in her hands. She'd told a whole lot of girls about Artie and they in turn could have told dozens of people. Bill might have heard the story from anybody—someone's boyfriend he'd met at work or someone's mother who'd served him in a shop. She thought of the posters plastered all over the place throughout the war, 'Careless Talk Costs Lives', and burst into tears.

Months later a batch of wedding photographs arrived from Oregon, followed by a string of breezily cheerful postcards. Then more photos—Artie and Virgie in the new Buick; Artie and Virgie on vacation in Florida; Virgie posed on some steps in her new fur coat …

LIZZIE AND THE GREAT OUTDOORS

Lizzie got hold of Fairy Twinkletoes, chopped her skirt to knee-length, took away her wand, pulled off the star and gave the silver stick to New Mowgli. Then she took her out to the garden to be New Mowgli's wife. In this role the poor thing led a wretched life. She had to carry the sack whenever New Mowgli went out foraging, gather the firewood, make the bed and cook all the food.

At nightfall New Mowgli would come back to his house and shout, 'Where are you, stupid Mrs Virgie? Where's my supper? Bring it here this minute you, selfish thing! It's self, self, self with you and I'm sick, weary and tired of it!'

And if Mrs Virgie failed to serve up something tasty New Mowgli would wallop her with a stick like Mr Punch in the Punch and Judy show Lizzie had seen once on the sands at Weston-Super-Mare.

But the following year, when Lizzie was nearly nine-years-old, Virgie sent her sister a frantic letter. It turned out that after Artie's business had gone bust he'd run away with Betty-Jo who'd worked in his drugstore, dispensing, to Lizzie's mother's surprise, not syrup of figs but coke and ice-cream sodas.

'She can't say I didn't warn her,' said Peg grimly. 'Alan Ladd, my foot.'

After that New Mowgli suddenly became a more considerate husband. He kissed Mrs Virgie on both cheeks and gathered her a great bouquet of scarlet blossoms, picked from the curling tendrils of Lizzie's father's beans as they reached towards the sky by the buddleia tree.

Philip Cox

My One True Love

How can I say otherwise? My one true love is architecture. This confession may be disappointing. Condemning other loves in my life. My children, my close friends, I love them too. Architecture absorbs my waking hours and my passion. On reflection I have treated others badly in my pursuit of adventure, that deep felt emotion I have for my art. I am completely at her mercy. Architecture is personified by female gender rather than masculine. It has been referred to at many times as the 'mother' of the arts because of its nurturing of painting, sculpture and craft. I am held within her motherly embrace.

Architecture gathers and girds herself with almost every aspect of life. It is the womb of life. Architecture encompasses space, it cradles life and all that civilisation provides and it is created by the child of that womb, the products of union between mind and matter.

Architecture is a lover who won't let up. Wherever I go buildings are assessed, appreciated, expelled or derided. I cannot move without being in her presence. I sit in a room and I assess the space, the textures, the forms, the materials, the details, the decoration, the furniture. I am excited, pleased, disappointed or repulsed by what surrounds me. My love has made me aware of advances by other architects. I am constantly evaluating my own philosophies and fidelity in contrast to others.

I suppose I was destined to fall in love with architecture. As a child we lived in an indifferent Californian bungalow at Killara in Sydney and was acutely aware of the limitations of that architecture with its bulbous squat columns and its short truncated gables. My mother and father had grown up in simple Georgian houses at Balmain and seemed indifferent to their habitat. Their great love was the garden and that tended to camouflage the mistakes of the early 1920 architecture. We were taken on walks around the bushland periphery of Killara on weekends, pedalling our bikes, or on the much adored scooter we would explore the new houses being built by architects such as Walter Bunning, Sidney Ancher, Kenneth Spain and John Brogan. We used to snigger at the 'Hollywood' nature of Brogan's work, mock Californian, mock Georgian, mock Tudor but revere the works of Ancher whose strong horizontal lines and columned verandahs and porches seemed so appropriate for the Australian bush. Ancher seemed to gently caress the bush with off-white, pale grey-green forms, flicking colour on an already established canvas of sage greens, greys and browns.

I announced in my later years at secondary school that I wished to become an architect much to the horror of my parents who had spent a fortune on private education and saw their investment evaporating. They urged me to reconsider—medicine or dentistry. I had the capacity and the intelligence they thought to do anything I wanted—but architecture! They had been through the depression and they knew what happened to architects—desperation and no work.

My love had already been kindled. The passions were rising in my bones. I would go for walks on my own through the bush, still existing in those days in pristine state with running streams and tall eucalypts in valley floors. Above on the sandstone ridges were tortured and sculptural forms of the *Angophora*, mixed amongst grass trees. The rock formations appeared to me like fortresses and walled cities of a former world. They grew out of the soil as an organic expression of some master architect. I had read some books by Frank Lloyd Wright and immediately understood his philosophy of an organic architecture—for there it was in the Sydney bushland in reality. There was the Australian Crak des Chevaliers, the Chartres Cathedral, the Acropolis. I had to search no further.

University in many ways was a disappointment. I had expected that my professors would have a passion for architecture, they had love, but passion? No. Excepting for Lloyd Rees—an artist employed by the Faculty to teach the history of art and instruct us in art classes. His love was not only for art, but for architecture. Architecture overwhelmed his paintings in the sixties of Tuscan hill villages and romantic cities on imaginary rivers lost in time and space. He venerated Chartres Cathedral as the greatest contribution to civilisation—a synthesis of art, painting, sculpture, stained glass windows and metalwork, with its soaring spaces transcending most earthly thoughts and matter, a tribute to the gods. He explained that love, although a constant emotion, was challenging, it could be questioned, it could be fickle, it may lead to disappointments, to frustration, but in the end love is enduring, forgives and accepts the idiosyncrasies of the other party. He was the only lecturer who could encourage and develop our love. Architecture gave me that inner swelling of human emotion, that burning excitement, that groggy head of desire, that tingling of erotic response which transcended reason and ultimately gave me the peace that passes all understanding.

After university I decided not to go to Europe immediately unlike my fellow students. My first job was designing a hostel for naughty boys and subsequently Tocal Agricultural College. It was extraordinary that my love had rewarded me. I spent most of my spare time writing a book with Max Freeland and going around rural Australia with Wesley Stacey photographing *Rude Timber Buildings*. It was in rural Australia that I found Australia's cathedrals—the woolsheds and the barns of the nineteenth century. Trunks of forest giants formed the naves and transepts of these wonderous buildings—medieval in their construction techniques. They imbued a spirit of strength and conveyed the essence of the bush, a calling into the spirituality of the country. I had a similar response when I eventually visited Lloyd Rees' Chartres; again when I glimpsed the Parthenon for the first time; and when I stood on the Pantheon on a rainy day seeing a pool of water on the marble floor, lit by a shaft of light from the ocular within the dome.

I am sure many Australians will say that the bush, the landscape of Australia are their true love. I too am thrilled by these like no other landscapes in the world, but I cannot see them except in architectural terms—line, shape, form, colour, texture, space—the essence of architecture.

Architecture succeeds when the spirit of place and landscape is imbued within it. When place and landscape are enriched by architecture, it is unthinkable to imagine that situation without architecture. Delphi, Mt Athos, the Potala, Acropolis, Sydney Opera House are some examples where the two lovers embrace and there is ecstasy and inevitable union between the natural and built environments.

Architecture is the measure of our times and our achievements. As civilisations rise and fall, architecture alone remains as evidence. It may be folly to imagine that our current civilisation will continue unabated. But future generations will find the ruins of our architecture, the crumbling spines of our cities, our bridges, the strange marks we left on the earth's crust and wonder at the technology which enabled them to happen. We look at the wonders of the ancient world with awe. Future generations will do exactly the same thing with our cities today.

My love for architecture is still intense, it remains my true love, my passion, my life. I cannot live without her. As I grow older, the mysteries of this love grow more intense while the forces ranged against us increase. Economic, social and political attitudes prevailing at particular times affect our love. There are seductive forces of money, position and power capable of corrupting this love and forces of self rebuke and criticism and the success that leads to being cut down in Australian society. These frustrations impact upon my ability to express feelings and thoughts within my art and articulating these in a meaningful way becomes more difficult. One becomes weary of the constant battle between those forces and the desire to produce the best possible result. We have many challenges in the production of architecture, however, provided that our love is sincere and remains intense, there is nothing to fear.

Despite all, there are opportunities for architecture to flourish in various scales from small works like a bus stand to large scale projects such as a football stadium.

My love for architecture has led me to exotic ports and has given me an understanding of South-East Asia culture where the genius of indigenous populations cherish the earth producing an architecture of extreme beauty and ingenuity. They have much to teach us of the harmonies of earth and nature.

Love can change over a lifetime. It can deepen when it is true. Many people fall out of love because the parties develop different directions and interests. The love generated between two is vulnerable to many forces and can only be sustained if it enriches itself by both parties having a devotion to each other and determination to be selfless in giving. Love withers when insensitive attitudes prevail and excitement and the longing for each other diminish.

    My true love is as stimulating, rewarding and exciting as it was in my first encounter. I am continually amazed at the variety of expression, the honesty and integrity of both sophisticated and primitive architecture, and the ecstasy of creation.

GARRY DISHER

Up Above the World

A pre-war Percival Gull has been found out there, lying broken-backed on a windless claypan, with a perfectly preserved corpse at the controls, and a dozen diamonds rattling around in a tobacco tin on the cockpit floor. A Gull, a corpse, and a dozen diamonds. An elegant conjunction of facts. And the location makes a kind of melancholy sense—an untravelled region of the Gibson Desert, between the Tropic of Capricorn and the Gunbarrel Highway. It all means that I can put a few things to rest, now, from the early weeks of 1942, when my brother washed back into my life and undid a little of the sufficiency I had found for myself.

This was near Broome, in the north-west, at the time of the invasion of Java, when Japanese bombs were falling like silver rain along the Kimberley coast and old certainties were crumbling, when desperate people, displaced by the chaos, were crossing land and sea in search of sanctuary, love and absolution.

In a sense, we were storm-tossed creatures. It was a season of storms, if sieges, land battles and aerial bombardments are reckoned along with torrential rain and the lash and mutter of changeable winds.

Records show that the wet of 1942 dumped twenty-eight inches of rain on us in just six weeks. Roads were washed away or impassable for days at a time. At Leeuwin Downs station, thousands of frogs and a chain of muddy lakes appeared. We dodged frogs, trod on them, awoke and went to bed with them. The skin of the earth seemed to crawl, tormented by their tiny pads. We sleepwalked through the enervating hours of daylight and slapped away the mosquitoes at night. Water seeped into the air raid shelter as quickly as we could pump it out. If fliers visited Leeuwin Downs, they'd skim the treetops first, to gauge the flood line on the airstrip, then splash down, skitter toward the leeward side of the hangar, and lash their little aeroplanes to the ground. There was always a gusting wind. You'd see the puny wings tremble like leaves.

This is a story about aeroplanes: love and aeroplanes. In 1925, when Rollo was eight and I four, our father took us to see Francesco de Pinedo land at Broome in a Savoia flying boat, in the final stages of a flight from Italy. Five years later, Rollo borrowed the tractor and cleared a landing strip on stony ground beyond our stockyards. By the time he was eighteen, he was enrolled at the Aero Club. Then our father bought him his first plane, a Gypsy Moth that had belonged to an oil company. You see, our mother had gone back to England, hating our father and possibly hating us. As a result, our father was inclined to spoil us.

You will want to know about Leeuwin Downs. You will want to know how big it was.

At a third of a million acres, it was one of the smallest along the Eighty Mile Beach. When you came to it through basalt outcrops and dry grass as high as a man's chest, it was like finding a village in the wilderness: main house, visitors' quarters, stockmen's quarters, storeroom, workshop, generator shed, stockyards, garden, windmill, iron Furphy tanks, airstrip.

In the mustering season we supported over thirty people. Five were European: Rollo, myself, our father, a bookkeeper, an engineer. The remainder were Aboriginal stockmen and domestic servants, and a community of local blacks who camped nearby for eight months of the year, and on ceremonial sites and hunting grounds during the wet when we had no work for them.

The house was large and cool, with handmade hardwood and crocodile hide chairs, a wine cellar, a Martini-Henry elephant rifle on the study wall, and a library furnished with books, armchairs and a piano. It wasn't an untidy house, but it did wear a faint patina of dust and neglect, as though my father stood in doorways from time to time and stared helplessly in upon the memories stored in unused rooms.

You could say that we belonged to a virtuous, powerful and mostly unaccountable elite. We dressed for dinner (a legacy of our mother), paid low wages to the stockmen and the gins, overstocked a vast tract of land with the wrong breed of cattle, and did nothing that might lower white prestige in the north.

Even so, *we* held the lease, not some absentee English landlord, and on my travels with Rollo I saw things that my father would never have countenanced: 'cheeky' stockmen forced to dress in women's clothing and do women's work; gins pulling a cord to fan the dinner table; floggings.

Rollo was not easy to love. He was a breezy, plausible charmer, who took risks and never came a cropper. He was offhand, careless, contestable, and fought bitterly with my father who knew him through and through, and tried to warn me, but I ignored him. Rollo made me pivotal in his adventures, and filled the gap left by our mother. If ever I felt resistance, it sat sourly in my stomach and diminished me in my own eyes.

I didn't mind that he wouldn't let me take off or land in the Moth. It was enough to feel the sensation of our passage through the air, the wind-nudge in the stick and the rudder, the dizzy risk of flying with a weakened strut or a bent tailwheel fork. I lived for our takeoffs from unfamiliar airstrips, the new day delivering us to a new horizon. We had no sense of danger. There were times when we put down on deserted beaches with engine trouble, but all I can remember of them is Rollo playing Gilbert and Sullivan on his portable gramophone and reaching into the engine bay with an oily rag, while sea birds wheeled against the blue sky.

When a sudden squall at Leeuwin Downs flipped the Moth onto its back, Rollo bought a Puss Moth, a high-winged monoplane with a sealed cockpit. Soon we were testing the limits of the new aeroplane, flying it to Wyndham, Roebourne, the Beagle Bay Mission, Darwin and twice across the Timor Sea to Koepang.

We became well-known in the north-west. We were a kind of travelling show. For three months in 1938, the Broome to Darwin record was ours. We searched for fliers lost in the desert country. We delivered the Royal Mail. We circumnavigated the continent twice. To mark Rollo's twenty-first birthday, we flew to Tjilatjap, on the island of Java, and holidayed at a hill station for ten days, indistinguishable from the colonial officials of Batavia in our white cotton.

• • •

One day I started a logbook, using it to describe terrain and landing conditions:

> Wyndham Aerodrome *Rollo calls it 'tenacious' and 'affectionate'. He means it's sticky when wet. It's about three miles long and known as a heat-generating saltpan.*

I was writing for myself, like a farmer who can't retire at night until he's licked his pencil stub and noted how many acres he's sown or lambs he's lost. But when Rollo began to rely on my reports as an aid to memory, I decided to elaborate upon them. I questioned mail pilots and station managers, and travelled many of the routes myself, by road. I noted pedal wireless frequencies so that we could call ahead for local weather reports. Where magnetic interference affected the compass, I suggested alternatives: *The woolshed at Mistake Springs has an east-west alignment.* I warned about the grass at Missiessy Station: *Radio to say you're coming so they can mow the strip.* I advised that the Derby pub closed for evening meals at six-thirty, and the use of a chamois filter when refuelling at Marble Bar.

They were home-grown observations. There was nothing shaped or formal about them. But they were serious. They were designed to save us from doing a perish.

We'd known for some time that Puss Moths were subject to wing distortion. An extra wing strut would have solved the problem, but when our father begged Rollo to attend to it, he brushed him aside. Perhaps he believed that his Puss Moth was one of the lucky ones, apt to become unlucky if he tampered with her, and so it was that one evening in March 1939, as we were landing in a cross-wind, a wing tore off and we cartwheeled into the ground.

Rollo escaped injury, but my leg was scraped raw and broken in several places. It's shorter than the other by an inch, now, which has skewed my lower back, so that I have lived in pain for most of my life, and it's thinner and terribly scarred. Nerve ghosts jump in it.

My father was furious. Rollo apologised to me, but bristled at my father, and asserted himself by buying another plane, a Percival Gull. She was lovely, a shapely, low-winged cabin monoplane fitted with a six-cylinder, air-cooled Gipsy Queen 2 motor that gave her a range of 640 miles at a cruising speed of 160 miles per hour.

Rollo said he was going to write his name into the record books. He'd tap his finger on aeronautical charts: 'Croydon, then Brindisi, Aleppo, Basra, Karachi, Calcutta, Rangoon, Singapore, Surabaya, Koepang and finally Wyndham.' Jean Batten had done it in just under six days in 1936, flying a Percival Gull. Rollo intended to fly the reverse route in five days, the round trip in ten.

But he didn't write himself into the record books. The war intervened. Rollo fretted, argued with my father, and a year later made his way to London to join the Royal Air Force.

Meanwhile I grew depressed. It was a problem of faith. The future offered me nothing except one unproductive year after another. The recruiting stations didn't want me. I felt fatigue, too, and anger, but more than anything a sense of insufficiency.

Then one day an RAAF officer landed at Leeuwin Downs on a tour of wartime airfields. He'd been told about my logbooks and wanted me to update and publish them for the RAAF. I would have a pilot to fly me up and down the coast. I felt useful again.

And the long silence between Rollo and my father ended. In May 1941, Rollo wrote to say that he'd been posted to Malaya. A flood of letters ensued. Rollo wrote once a week, my father several times, but letter time is ordered differently from real time. It's rarely linear and responsive. Some of these letters failed to arrive, others arrived out of sequence or weeks late. An anxious query might be met by an apology, a declaration by a reproval. It was a contestable correspondence, reflecting their similar temperaments and difficult history. But it also reflected their love, as if Rollo no longer blamed our father for driving our mother away.

I believe, too, that he was afraid. By January 1942, the allies were no longer holding against the Japanese in Malaya. Troops and refugees crossed the causeway on to Singapore Island. Rabaul fell on 23 January, Ambon on 2 February. Then Singapore surrendered. Darwin was bombed. Clearly, the Japanese did not have weak eyesight. Their planes were not constructed of bamboo and ricepaper.

At night I worked on my logbooks while my father listened to the Department of Information broadcasts. I can still recall the uninflected, well-bred voices (tweed-coat-pipe-in-the-corner-of-the-mouth kinds of voices), the darkness outside, windows masked with black bituminous paper, the wireless, and my father, tense in his chair:

> *The principle of white Australia shall never be overturned by armed aggression. The Japanese violate our deepest and most fundamental instincts, and we shall not rest until they have been cleared from the earth.*

Once a Japanese spotter plane buzzed us. The next day a Qantas pilot landed with Dutch refugees from Batavia. He had ten minutes of fuel left. We filled his tank from Rollo's drums and watched him struggle to clear the trees.

Then one evening in early March we heard the heavy drone and counter-beat of twin aero engines. As I listened, one motor stuttered and cut out, and before I could find my stick, the other motor cut out.

I limped from the house. A silver Lockheed Electra, with the Netherlands triangle on its tail and wings, was making a steep, tilted, powerless landing approach over the airstrip. I cried, 'Straighten up'.

I tracked the Lockheed's graceless descent below the tree line, tensing for the impact. There was a crack as the right landing strut broke. The Lockheed spun around, slicing the right wing off on a tree. Then silence. No dust. No explosions or screaming. The Lockheed simply lay belly down in the red mud. That's when I noticed a stitching of bullet holes across the fuselage.

A door opened. Rollo stepped out.

Now when I recreate that day and the next, and the visit by detectives a week later, and by a Changi survivor at the end of the war, I can see why Rollo behaved so oddly.

First there was his indifference to the wounded passenger, a Dutch colonial official. The man's wife and baby were dead in their seats. Rollo's navigator died of wounds before we could free him. But the Dutchman, although unconscious, would live, if we could get him to a hospital. Rollo, dark eyed with exhaustion, seemed more intent upon unloading the luggage.

Then he wanted us to dismantle and burn the Lockheed. He was quite panicky. 'If a Jap spots us, he'll treat us as a legitimate target.'

We did as we were told, but my father didn't like it. He wanted simply to help the Dutchman, embrace Rollo, hear all of his stories.

Then there was Rollo's manner: edgy, easily spooked, hunted-looking. We put it down to his recent experiences. He told us over supper that he'd escaped from Singapore on a freighter. When it was torpedoed, he swam ashore and bribed a fisherman to take him to Java. There the Dutch asked him to ferry refugees to Australia. 'My first trip, and I strike a pair of Zeros.'

You can sense it when a cyclone is building. It's as if your skin is charged.

The next morning, compelled by the premonitory cast of the light, I rapped my knuckles on the barometer and watched the needle calibrate the day closer to a storm front. The house felt as tight as a drum around me. The air outside was very still, but I saw a willy-willy, a small, whipping funnel of dust and grit that immediately lost itself, almost as if it had been imagined, and I knew that a storm was brewing.

My father felt it too. He finally stuck out his jaw and said, 'Look, Rollo, that Dutch fellow needs a hospital. Take him in the Gull. You'll be back in no time. I even radioed to say you were coming.'

Rollo went white. 'You interfering old bugger.'

That's the last thing he said to my father. But he did take the wounded man in the Gull. Later I discovered that he'd also taken my logbooks.

When he didn't return, we wondered if he'd crashed. It was a vicious cyclone, after all, lasting sixteen hours and uprooting trees and tearing off our roof. My father died a little when Rollo didn't come back. According to the detectives, a week later, Rollo did make it to the hospital at Marble Bar, but where was he now, and where were the diamonds of the Netherlands Government?

You could say that my brother had an opportunistic war. A man turned up in 1945 with an IOU in Rollo's handwriting. He wanted a thousand pounds. He said a thousand pounds was poor recompense for finding women's clothing for Rollo and smuggling him aboard a ship bound for Batavia. 'That could have been me,' he said. 'Three years I spent in Changi.' My father paid, just to be rid of the poor wretch, and died a little more inside.

I shouldn't think that Rollo hurt anyone; I might have run, if I'd been in his shoes. But his slipperiness, and our never seeing him again, or knowing what had happened to him, destroyed my father and me.

The thing is, when I think of my logbooks now, all I can see is a failure of language and imagination. You'd not know, from my descriptions, that the desert slipping by beneath the cockpit can exact a penalty; that evening falls rapidly on deserted beaches, bringing whispers and deep, moonspot shadows; that an escarpment may be a place of locked-in secrets and malign intent; that size is not liberating but claustrophobic.

Sometimes I'd specified roofs and fences simply to distinguish unvarying terrain. Nothing is particular, all is general, out there. Dunes fold into dunes, savannah into savannah, in meaningless, hypnotic multiples. That's where the things that vanish find a resting-place. It's easier nowadays. You make your cartographic marks and write in the yellow emptiness: *designated remote area.*

And I'd looked over the side of the cockpit and used other people's memories, their frustrations, disappointments and lickspittling: 'Mistake Creek', for example. 'Point Torment'. 'Prince Regent River'. And what did Warrawagine mean? Good tucker? The place where the serpent coils asleep? Some explorer's approximation of the local expression for 'Piss off'?

But there were layers of memory that I hadn't reached. A bay is always more than just a bay. It's where the frog swallowed all of the waters of the world. Macassan sailors fished it for *bêche-de-mer*. A Dutch merchantman anchored there in 1631. It's named for a rich patron in London. Four black women were raped and murdered there by Japanese pearlers in 1926. It's where Rollo and I dragged the Puss Moth free of the creeping tide.

It's as if I'd written about a country outside of my experience, even though I'd grown up on the margins of it. Or rather, I'd lived in a place and imagined it at the same time. The imagined coastline, desert and savannah constituted the better place, but, in being imagined, it shape-slipped and dissolved. I had never reached it, yet it's where I lived. That disappointment has stayed with me for all my life.

Rosie Scott

Grace

At the beginning of the wet season, Grace saw something which kept tormenting her, a sight which she couldn't dismiss from her mind. In a grove by the sea, just off the Ara Tapu she noticed a child's skull lying by a tree, earth clinging to its eye sockets. As she stood there she was suddenly made aware that there were ancient bones and skulls everywhere, scattered among the rocks and ploughed-up earth where the bulldozer had been. She stood very still, listening to the murmur of the sea, the cicadas clicking in the pandanus, her heart beating so painfully she felt as if her chest could burst.

After that she went up to the water gardens in the Takuvaine Valley nearly every afternoon for comfort, and lay on the grass by the pools, half-drowning in the heat, pretending to sleep. She flung out her arms and legs like a child and covered her face with one hand though she was lying deep in the shade. The air was filled with the murmur of water; it was a cool, ancient place with grass as smooth as lawn spreading to the water's edge, and teitei trees shading the pools. The water brimmed over into channels smothered with ferns and moss, it gleamed, half-hidden under the heart-shaped taro leaves. Once she followed the stream up into the jungle to its source, the old paths there were worn so deep by generations of feet that they were half underground, a silent green world.

The presence of the past was everywhere, she had a sense of the people who coaxed the shimmering system down the hills all those centuries ago, their descendants who came to plant taro and gossip in the shade, the birds once flew in dazzling flocks in the jungle. She knew about the birds because an old man told her about them when she was a child, he imitated their calls for her and lovingly described their plumage by showing her the pearly inside of a shell and a poinciana flower. As a little girl she imagined them bright as peacocks, darting through the trees. The gardens had always been her favourite place, she loved dreaming there, thinking of nothing, lulled by the singing water, with only the old soothing voices of the past for company.

There was an invasion of butterflies that month because of the unusual heat, no-one had ever seen so many in Rarotonga before. All through the wet season they drifted on iridescent wings high up in the trees, they floated dreamily in the sea-green light of the jungle. Up in the water gardens they were so thick that gazing up at them in the tree tops made her dizzy. She felt stretched thin enough to be dissolved like vapour into that desirable half-lit world. In the mornings, before the rain, families came up to the gardens to plant taro in their pools. They stood knee-deep in the water talking in low voices, but by afternoon they were all gone and everything was still, beaten flat by the fiery heat. The only moving things were the butterflies dancing on the surface of the pools.

Sometimes when it was too hot to walk up the valley she sat on the verandah of their house instead and dozed there, not moving for hours, her straw hat tilted over her eyes. It was like going up a tropical river, trees pulsing and glittering on its hazy banks, the cat purring beside her as they travelled through the afternoon. But always, wherever she was, when she finally woke, it returned, and her mind started circling again, round the scene of desecration, the pity of the pathetic bones, her shameful inability to do anything.

'You remind me of a Southern belle out there. All pale and soft and melted in the heat. Complicated internally. Waiting for the beau who never comes,' her mother said, trying to be friendly. 'So this is your life, my girl, working in the biggest hole in Avarua and dreaming your life away.' She was wearing a housecoat, her hair pinned up, she was beautiful with violet shadows under her eyes from a lifetime of sleepless nights.

They had lived together for years in this house, with the mynahs squawking outside in the flame trees, and the Rua Manga towering in the distance above the jungle. Grace thought there was something beautiful and momentous about the wild clearing, the house with its rough walls long ago stripped of paint by the sun. Nothing had been touched on it for years, it had become a magnificent setting for her mother's passionately misspent life. Inside, the rooms were high-ceilinged and bare, the video flickered in the lounge day and night. The greenish light poured into the room so that it was like living inside an aquarium. Here her mother sat out her days, watching videos and drinking, great jungle insects crawling silently up the walls.

'It's not an active life,' she told her daughter, 'but I'm biding my time.'

'For what?' asked Grace, knowing too well.

'I'd leave this place tomorrow, Grace. Your grandfather says he is going to come up with the money. For a few thousand dollars I'd fly out on the next plane dragging you with me. We'd go back to Auckland, buy a little cottage in a proper suburb and then your life would begin.'

'There must be something you like about the life here,' Grace said. 'You've been here long enough.'

'Not a thing,' said Mara, and Grace looked lovingly out into the trees as if someone was calling her from there.

'You've never had any ambition at all,' her mother said. 'When I was your age I was preparing for university. Mostly languages. And of course I'd met my husband-to-be, your father, and such an eligible young man required a lot of tactics. Trips abroad too. I want you to have all that.'

Grace had her own private allegiances, though she never would have said so. She knew the island was her only home, and a precious source of comfort. She had never had any friends, because of her perilous, uncomfortable life with her mother, so she had learnt to stay loyal only to what she saw in front of her …

'Bleeding heart,' her mother called her, especially when she was half-drunk and maudlin about the injustices in her life. Bleeding heart. The image was so savage it made Grace feel sick to hear it. She could see the blood draining away from her poor dying heart and no-one there to stop the flow.

All through the wet season, the thought of the papa'a (white people) builders pouring concrete on the bones and then building the motel step by step on top of them nagged at her. She dreamt of some violent unmasking which would shock the people into claiming back their dead. Every night after work, she had to walk home along the Ara Tapu and pass the shell of the half-built motel. The jungle crowded right up to the road in the darkness there and the huge mass of rustling, scented, secret life blotted out the memory of the whining saws, the bulldozer, the traffic as if they had never existed.

Walking silently down the road, she was swallowed up by the softness, the infinity of the Pacific. The jungle, the endless pain of murmuring dark sea, the depths of the tropical night sky seemed to go on forever and merge, their patient immensity as familiar and troubling to her as a dream landscape. The darkness was heavy with life, the presence of long-forgotten people and vanished worlds. There was a sadness about it which filled her with pity and fear as she tried to slip past the site unnoticed, she knew there was very little time left.

'You know yourself, Grace, that you'll never do anything here,' her mother told her, justifying herself. She had come in early one morning and sat weeping on the bed, the cheque from her father in her hand.

'But I'm not leaving,' said Grace coldly.

'The old son of a bitch,' her mother said. 'Finally come up with it, but not for me. And you don't want it. The irony of it. But you're just going to have to take it. I won't rest till you do.'

Grace wanted to hit her, she imagined her mother's thin alcoholic bones cracking. But she knew once she'd started there would be no end to her rage against the world. She was frightened by her own intensity, the ache of loss, her fear.

'Leave me alone,' she said half to herself and ran out of the house. When she reached the water gardens her body was shining with sweat, she was at the limit of her endurance. She felt like a sleepwalker who had just been woken roughly and was staring in horror at her new surroundings. It was as if she was being allowed a brief glimpse of the mysterious connections running through the world, at the point where the past and future met and nothing was as it seemed.

The silent invasion of butterflies, flickering like spirits in the leaves, she saw suddenly for what it really was—a commemoration of all the lost creatures of the island, living and dead, and a warning for anyone who would listen. For the first time too she could see the people who built the water gardens, as plainly as old friends. They worked beside her, their garden growing under their hands as naturally and peacefully as a waterfall. They were making it to feed their people and she knew, watching them, that it was a work of perfect love. She realised that it was their bones she had seen scattered so cruelly in the earth, in the place where they were once laid to rest with loving ceremony.

She lay back on the grass and shut her eyes tightly against all this, she did not want to see any more. But as she lay there, through the darkness of her clenched eyelids she saw them, coming so sweetly, the lost birds, crying and swooping through the trees, their wings flashing like tongues of fire.

MEME McDONALD

The Vine

Holidays are hard. I'm going to make this one easy. Just Pete and me. No kids, no organising, no decisions. I booked a tour, accepted my dear mother-in-law's offer, and left the three kids at home. Sophie's the youngest. Thirteen. A handful. We need a break from each other.

A package tour. Ten-day Red Centre Experience, Uluru, Kata Tjuta, Kings Canyon, MacDonnell Ranges, luxury resort accommodation some of the time, twelve-star camping the rest. Reward yourself, the brochure says, with an outback escape. I never thought I'd do it. I hate that word 'outback'. That's where I grew up and to me it wasn't out the back of anywhere. It was my home, the centre of the world.

But we're here. We made it. We've arrived. Dinner's done. Pete's gone to bed. The meeting-new-people smile washes off my face along with the make-up and I settle into the quiet. My holiday's begun.

I can't sleep. I open the doors on the desert night. The smell of cool evening air sinking into the hot earth makes me want to dance or weep or walk naked into the night and never come back. Instead, I drag a chair outside and sit, trying to make out that shape in the dark, the one big one, the one living breathing mountain of a shape—Uluru.

I notice my breathing change, become slow and easy. I've got space for me. I don't know what I want to do first. I'm getting tingly in all kinds of places. I can't imagine lying straight in bed. I still feel a bit wobbly. I don't know if you've had that feeling when you can't tell if the car's stopped, the movement keeps going. Or when you jolt awake in the night, something cramping in on you. You can't go back to sleep because you can't trust that you'll wake up. I've had the tests. All clear. But I know there's something growing in there.

I need a holiday is all anyone can tell me. They're right. Even at the airport check-in, I felt the responsibilities lift off my shoulders like baggage, rolling away down the conveyor belt and into the belly of this big bird, this cocoon about to carry me away for a rest from my life. I even got the giggles, girl giggles, silly giggles over nothing more than the airline stewards' safety demonstration.

Looking down on the dot-painted landscape moving in giant serpent trails and caterpillar ridges, I thought of the country I grew up in. Flat, dry country. Red earth between clumps of mulga trees. Next thing I'm crying, trying to figure out why I feel like I'm an outcast.

I'm always searching for landmarks to make sense of who I've become. Staring into the dark, trying to make out shapes. In the middle of the night, that's what cramps in on me. I try to relax, to hold my mind still. You start delving into those dark places and you don't know if you'll ever come out alive. I close the doors on the desert night and get ready for bed.

Tonight, I'm not wearing pyjamas. I haven't done this in years. I'm naked. The chill of fresh sheets makes my skin tingle. I love Pete's warm smell. It reminds me of long nights and late mornings making love an age ago. I want more of that smell and I curve in close to him. The flannelette of his pyjamas tickles. I go to slip my hand beneath the elastic of his pants and lift his shirt to feel his bare back, to rub my breasts against him and stroke strong thighs …

I roll over. It's never as good as my dreams. Still, I'm going to lie here naked all night. I might wake up with a back chill or a sore throat but for once in my life I'm going to worry about that when it happens, not now. Now I'm going to lie back and dream and feel my own places and stroke them with fantasies that flicker and dance even after years of replay.

No sore throat. No chill. The desert morning is crisp and I'm alive. And there it is. Uluru. I can feel a throb begin inside as sweet as two hearts in love.

I climb onto the bus along with the rest of our tour group. We bounce over to the base of the Rock like a mob of school kids in a foreign country. My loose-mouth chatting about nothing to everybody has stopped. I can't find much to say this morning. I want to take things slowly.

We join a plague of other tourists. Our group is discussing who wants to climb up, who will go first, how many people have fallen and died, who's had a by-pass or a triple by-pass or their whole bloody heart transplanted. I feel the vine growing stronger round my heart till it hurts. The throb of this big, red mountain makes me melt to the size of an ant. I have to get closer.

Voices fade away. There's just me and this. Its skin is brittle, willing to crumble to dust with the touch of a finger. Yet the strength below feels enough to keep the heartbeat of a whole world pumping. My hand pulls back. Is it right just to walk up and touch? I don't know. The others are moving on. Pete's coming across to get me. I give him a wave. I want to stay here. I can't tell him why I don't want to climb up. I'll be fine, I say. I'll meet you back at the hotel if I get sick of waiting. You go with the others. He gives me a hug and I watch us draw apart like two astronauts walking on the surface of the moon.

The sun is baking. I follow the morning air as it retreats into shadows deep in the folds of rock. I find a spot to rest in the cool. Back to back, I lean ever so carefully against this huge heart. I need a transplant. I'm only half joking. I stare up into the blue, looking for answers.

I pull my thoughts back down to earth but they fly off again like balloons caught in a wind tunnel. The secrets of a thousand souls swirl all around. This kind of place makes you religious. Prayers fly up before you can stop them. I want to cry but if I do I know I will never stop. Inland Sea Rises Again. I can see the headlines. I hurry out into the sun.

The light is blinding. Troops of buses empty out their cargo of camera clickers on solid ground. I want to be a part of them. I latch onto a group headed back to the Visitors' Centre. I need a cuppa, an excuse to sit down in the bustle of other people's lives. I want the structure of labels and prices, hot chips a dollar fifty, and four walls. Maybe I'm dehydrated. Lost and thirsty in the middle of my own desert.

There's a group of Aboriginal people outside. They are demonstrating some of their crafts. Women are weaving grasses, children are being children, and one man, a middle aged man, a man about my age holds a boomerang in his hand. His fingers caress the wood. His skin is dark and at home in the sun. I long for the touch of that hand. I know that hand. I feel giddy. I'm losing it. I'm an embarrassment to myself. I've got to find Pete.

The touch of that hand is stuck to me. I can't find my way out of this place. Everywhere I turn there's glass, walls of glass squashing me into a reflection. I remember how he smiles. I run outside. It's hot. It's too far to go back. There's no bus. Pete! I'm calling out, running, crying. I fall hard. I'm thirteen again, with a grazed knee. I want my mum to pick me up, to tell me she loves me, to bathe my wound and smooth ointment on the sore bits to take away the pain.

I lie in the dirt. A grown woman, a white woman, crumpled and covered in dust. Grief rolls through me like thunder. I give in to the storm. The throb of that heartbeat comes up through the earth. It pulls the tears down my face in rivers of mud. A fresh smell lifts in the air from this first rain falling on hot earth. I look up. I can see across to where steel poles and rattling chains guide explorers up the great body of rock. I hope Pete and the others take their time coming back.

That night I sleep naked again. In the morning I explain to Pete that I need to stay here today. I can't go on the day trip to Kata Tjuta. I have to sort myself out. Acclimatise. He's getting pissed off. He gets that way when he's worried. It's like an equal and opposite reaction. I ask him just for this one day. I know I'm stretching it. Maybe it's menopause, I joke. At least that gives us a laugh.

I kiss Pete and wave the four-wheel drive goodbye. A cloud of dust carries me across to the Visitors' Centre. The women weaving aren't there, nor are the children being children, and the man, the man isn't there. I'll wait. It's still early. A log lies, silver grey, in the place where they were sitting yesterday. I sit with my back to the sun and feel at home. My fingers reach for a twig and start drawing in the dry earth. Two figures, a boy and a girl, curly hair, fingers on hands, holding hands. How do you make figures in the dirt have different coloured skin?

Little feet appear at the top of my drawing, small bare toes. The children have come. And the women. I'm in their place. They're looking down at me, friendly, curious smiles, interested to see what I've been drawing. I offer a weak good morning. The man, the man has come. He's standing behind them. Looking up, I feel like a teenager, lost for words.

THE VINE

With a wipe of a shoe, I rub my doodles back into the earth. The women look at me with sorry eyes.

Can I talk to you, I ask the man? My words flap in the breeze, awkward as undies on a line. He takes his time to answer. Yep. Thank God. I want to do something stupid like hug him. He's probably seen a lot of us crazy whitefellas. I keep going. Can I get you a cup of tea? Can we sit down in the cafe? I hope you don't mind me asking so much of you but there is something very important I want to speak to you about. He doesn't answer but leads the way to the cafe.

Every table looks exposed. We sit uncomfortably and wait for the tea and raisin toast I ordered. Would you mind if I hold your hand? I had to ask. I've gone past the point of worrying what anyone thinks including this man who is being so patient. I look at our hands together, the paleness wrapped against the brown, the dark brown. The map of our lives crisscrossing the palms, the same pink palms. The beauty of our two hands holding is enough. This is worth making an idiot of myself.

A young girl with a smirk on her face slaps the plate of raisin toast down. Sharing are we? I nod. White tea with two sugars, butter melting on hot bread, smells warming the air, these things give me strength. I try speaking. I'm forty-nine. My voice sounds different. The man drinks his tea. I'm married. I have three children. I go on with the recipe of my life, hoping the list of ingredients will identify who I am as much for me as for this kind stranger. I live in Melbourne now. I haven't always lived in Melbourne. I grew up out west in New South Wales near a little place called Gadunga. We lived on a property, sheep and cattle. He's looking at me. His dark eyes have softened. Maybe he's wondering what it would be like to be a lost soul.

I grew up in country a bit like this. I spent a lot of time by myself as a kid in the bush. I'd pack a paper bag full of homemade bickies and sandwiches and ride my horse across the open paddock. I was only seven or eight. I'd head for a sand hollow in the middle of a clump of trees. It'd be cool in there, shady. That's when I'd feel those spirits all around, but I didn't know what to call that feeling then. I never knew any of the stories of my place. I miss home.

I went to school in town. I describe the swimming pool and the picture theatre, the pubs and the one Greek cafe. All the places that blacks and whites were segregated from each other not by laws like South Africa, not laws that could be written up on walls and ripped down. These laws were imprinted on the minds of each child from birth. White is good and clean and the colour of angels. Black is bad and dirty and sinful. Never the twain shall meet.

George and I did meet. Our eyes met waiting for the school bus, at little lunch, across the football field, walking down the street, leaving the picture theatre. When our eyes met it was with love and longing to be together. It was so strong it pushed and pulled us around until one day after school there we were, behind the corner store, face to face, hand in hand, breathing close. His body was warm, his smell was good. When he touched me it was with care, not grabbing. We kissed in the way of first ever kisses. Small and quick but enough to make our hearts burst open and flow together in a rush. I wanted us to keep holding onto each other forever. We missed the bus.

All hell broke loose. Not right then because of course I made up a story as to why I missed the bus and it wasn't anything to do with George. But soon, in the rush that young love has of living a lifetime in a day, I couldn't hold my love in. Mum and I were pegging out the clothes. I'd been really helpful round the house since I was breaking all the rules everywhere else. Mum was asking me about the pictures. I'd lied to her, you see. I'd said I was going with my friend and her aunty. I met George inside. We sat downstairs in the canvas seats, holding hands. The warmth of our two hands together made the world perfect. We didn't do much more than that on the scale of one to ten. I didn't think that anyone from upstairs, where us white people usually sat, would see me. They must have. Someone must have said something to Mum. She was like a dog with a bone, tight and determined. She wouldn't stop asking questions.

Before I knew what had happened, his name was out there, hanging off the line, in full view. George ... Mum didn't wait for the surname.

It was like riding your bike full pelt into the door of a truck that swings open in front of your face. Mum's response was so immediate, so harsh and so unrelenting that I was thrown to the ground. I feared for my life. Every emotional bone in my body was broken. I had no way to stand up and be strong and speak out against the things that Mum and Dad said about boongs and abos and no-good drunks. They would never allow a girl

The Vine

of theirs to get mixed up with a bunch of blackfellas, they said. Why, they asked, would a clever girl like you want anything to do with a mob of no-hopers anyway?

I didn't answer. My mouth went dry. I couldn't talk.

It took me a long while to learn to walk again, you know, to feel confident in yourself, to want to go on with life. As soon as I finished school, I moved away to the city, became a nurse, met Peter, got married, had kids, got a dishwasher. I live a comfortable life.

Coming out here has stirred it all up again. Your hand, I think about his hand stroking my face. I wonder about a different way of life. Mostly, I wonder why I never stuck up for him. I was only thirteen, I know, but I've never stuck up for him since, either. Every time I go back home, something comes up about Aboriginal people. I freeze. I can't talk. At dinner parties and work functions, I hear these silly comments. Everyone has a theory, an opinion. In some people, fear makes them hard and dangerous. I change the subject. I hear my nice voice disappear off into weather reporting and talking about kids.

That's why this vine is killing me, this vine wrapping around my heart. We've been a long time holding hands, this man and I. I don't know how much of this I've said in words and how much was a meeting of our minds. I try to lighten up. When they lay me out, do you think they'll put it down to a heart attack, I ask him? I'm nearly fifty. I'm the age for it. Is this what happens? Can you die of a broken heart?

He doesn't answer. He knows I'm not really joking. He looks into my heart for himself. Then he tells me a story. The story is about wrong love, of going against the wishes of your tribe. I travel through this spirit world, smoothing his words on old wounds like a rare ointment. This story makes sense of my life. It lets me forgive myself. Tears wash down my cheeks, flooding the table.

We sit in silence. His hand holds mine in the way I remember. Finally, he speaks. That one there, that love of yours, that one true love. He don't need a body to hold him. That fella's with you anyway. But that fear, that one growing round your heart, he's got to find a way out. You keep pretending and pretending and he'll climb all over you. You'll be gone.

I prayed today, I tell him. I don't do that often. Not to any particular God. In the shadows of Uluru I prayed to meet George again before I die.

I'm talking and crying at the same time. I've never been able to do that. My prayer is answered, I tell him. Thank you. Our two hands wash together and become rock. My words are slow and I can feel them carry all that I want to say. Thank you for listening to me. From my heart I tell him other things that don't need words to carry. I thank him for giving me back my voice, for making me gentle with myself, for saving my life. His reply stops me from going on. You listened to this place with this one here. He points to my heart. That's why I sat down with you. That's what makes this tea and this toast here taste good.

I walk with him back to the others. We hug and say goodbye. As I turn to go, the man passes me something. Take that one with you. It will make you stand up strong, he says. The boomerang is carved smooth, the wood rich, decorated with the markings of its long life. You are welcome here anytime, he says as I leave. Thank you for respecting our place.

Rain falls on the land that afternoon. Like the Gods or the Ancestors or the whole of that other world is mourning for love lost, for opportunities missed, for the pain of living with lies and misunderstanding and the torture of wrong doing. Torrents of rain wash over Uluru that night. The rain is unusual for this season, they reckon, but spectacular as always.

This night I sit and write. The story I'm writing is to go with the boomerang, to be passed down to my kids and theirs. I hope Peter wants to read it. Mostly, it's my way of saying sorry to George for not sticking up for us. Our paths may have gone different ways, but I owed it to us both to stand my ground, to honour our love. Thirty-six years later, I'm finally sticking up for love. No more silence. No more lies to eat at my heart.

My old pyjamas are cosy. I slide into bed and wrap myself close to Peter. On the edge of sleep I smell the sweetness of desert blossoms flowering on a vine.

DON DUNSTAN

My One True Love

How did it all begin? For my love is constant, unfailing, rewarding, providing ongoing sensual and intellectual satisfaction, interest and delight, a vehicle for demonstrating affection, a means of communication and closeness, a haven from the stresses of life. How often can that be said of other loves?

My childhood interest in food was not very different, I suppose, from that of other children except that growing up as I did in Fiji, as well as country South Australia, gave me a broader and more diverse experience of foods and tastes than others of my age.

Although I had the usual childhood suspicions of tastes I did not know beyond the nursery, in Fiji, as a small boy there was the constant challenge of the new. I readily accepted the fruits I grew up with in our little sugar mill town—bananas were a favourite (I loved them mashed with sugar). There was always papaya with lime juice for breakfast and I feasted on pineapples, mangoes, tropical mandarins, passionfruit and grenadillas. I learned to love the fresh river fish and the wonderful taste of mudcrabs caught in the estuaries.

Since I had eaten it from the hands of my Fijian nursegirls as a baby I could feast on the staple Fijian starch food—dalo—(a grey-fleshed taro which they simply boiled and fed me in gooey lumps) although objectively it really tastes like soap! I was to learn that many cultures have a starch base for peasant and infant food which is pretty tasteless; grits in the United States of America, mealy-mealy in Africa, sago mash in Niugini, though porridge in Britain and congee in China have rather more taste than the others.

My father kept a poultry yard and we usually had a roast duck or fowl stuffed with sage and onion for Sunday lunch—my little saliva glands started into action when that was brought to the table. But I firmly rejected some of the horrors of food served up by Australians and New Zealanders living in Fiji. Going to boarding school in Suva at the age of six, I had to live in an establishment run by an elderly spinster called Miss Grayburn. It was very spartan. The vegetables were all boiled and while I had been used to boiled dalo, boiled breadfruit, was and remains, for me excessively unattractive.

I got into serious trouble with the old martinet when, on one occasion, she served some re-cooked meat, minced and made into patties she called 'rissoles'. They smelled awful to me. I took one small taste and put my knife and fork down and sat without eating further.

'Donald,' she said 'eat up your nice rissoles.'

I had been taught strictly to be a polite and respectful child and simply said, 'No thank you, Miss Grayburn.'

'Why don't you like them?'

This was too much for me. 'They taste to me like dead horseflesh,' I said. I was in disgrace for weeks. But my determination to exercise judgement about food was strengthened.

After those weeks I caught a very serious streptococcus infection. I became seriously ill, but was eventually cured after months in bed with the careful ministrations of my mother (antibiotics were then, of course, unknown) and was eventually sent to Australia to live with my widowed grandmother and my aunts in Murray Bridge.

It was there that quite new experiences of food started to delight me. My mother's people had descended from farmers and had retained the habit of growing food for the table. The garden of my grandmother's house had fruit trees—two apricots, two peaches, a navel and a Seville orange, a luscious nectarine and a fig, grapevines of sultana and muscatel. All of these were new to me and in the season I sat in the trees and gorged myself—the wonderful flavours of the developed fruits of Europe filled me with delight. When asked what I would most like to eat the answer was always 'fruit salad'.

Our neighbours also had good fruit trees and in addition to the kinds in my grandmother's garden, they had three varieties of plums. My great aunt Eve lived only half a kilometre away and she had currants, raisins and sultanas which she dried and used in the rich fruit cakes and buns she baked. She had a number of almond trees and I helped to knock down the almonds when they were ready and spread their husks out to dry in the sun so the kernel could be put to storage. One of my earliest lessons about preparing food was to shell and blanch almonds ready for her cakes.

Murray Bridge is a town where many of the Lutheran refugees from Silesia settled and in those days, their German cultural background was obvious. In the 1930s, they still spoke their own dialect of German at home and many of them only spoke English with a strong German accent. In our little street there were six families—and three of them were German, as were our neighbours to the rear. So Murray Bridge had German bakeries and as I walked from school to my aunt's shop at lunchtime I smelt the wonderful scent of freshly baked breads and yeast cakes rich in cinnamon and nutmeg.

Every year, my family went to a feast put on in Monarto (where my great-great grandparents had settled in 1840) by the Laws sisters—three spinster ladies of Scottish descent who were members of my Aunt Eve's Presbyterian church. This feast was a church celebration. The Laws sisters farmed their land, milked their cows, separated the milk, and served up quite the best shortbread I have ever had and freshly baked scones with their own jams and lashings of rich whipped cream. Now that was food about which there was never a polite refusal from me (at least until I could manage no more).

At home with grandmother, however, sometimes there was. She was then semi-invalid, and so did little of the cooking. My aunts went out to work in the family business, so the house was cared for and most of the cooking done by a live-in maid. My aunt's taste in food—no doubt learned from her mother—was for plain cooking. My Aunt Beth always proudly proclaimed, 'We had nothing but the best—nothing but roasts and grills.' They were always overdone, and she might have added boiled and baked vegetables, and occasionally so-called salad, which was shredded lettuce with sliced tomato and pickled beetroot.

They had great difficulty then in getting me to eat boiled brussels sprouts (as they would today) and my sense of the need to discriminate was again reinforced by some of the puddings that appeared. One night we were sitting at the table and the maid brought in a 'Queen's pudding'. This was a confection of stale sponge cake cut in pieces, covered with an egg custard (which the maid always managed to curdle) then covered with a layer of jam and spread with beaten egg white and browned while leaving the egg white uncooked. I didn't like it and when my aunt offered a generous plateful I said, 'No thank you, Aunty.'

'Oh but it's lovely, Dondies.'

'No thank you, Aunty.'

My aunt, who knew that I, aged eight, had been reading A. A. Milne, said 'Oh what's the matter with Mary Jane—it's nice rice pudding again?' She was cajoling me—unsuccessfully. 'No thank you, Aunty.' My Aunt accepted defeat and served my grandmother and herself. My grandmother, who was short-sighted, took a good spoonful, put it in her mouth and exploded with indignation. 'It's not rice pudding!' she cried. I nearly fell off my chair laughing. I couldn't have liked it more!

But I did learn something from grandmother which I would later undertake myself. To keep fruits that were in season for more than just fruit salad, my great-aunt and most of our neighbours dried some. But grandmother and some other people we knew bottled fruit—usually in syrup. They used a Vacola outfit to ensure that the fruit was not wasted but provided fruit for desserts and morning cereals. I helped peel and place fruit in the jars—although I was still only mildly interested in the processes that led to eating good food.

Returning to Fiji at age ten I could now, with the road improved, live with my parents and go to school daily in Suva. I was plunged back into a very different society and very different food. My parents had shielded me from spices like pepper or chillies. They did no longer. I used to go to the Nausori market and walk down the main street of town. One's nostrils were immediately assaulted by the smells of Indian and Chinese cooking. Clove, coriander, cumin, turmeric, cardamom and mustard all combined with the smell of sandalwood incense to make a heady mix of aromas.

To enlarge my father's income beyond his salary as manager of the local firm of general merchants, he was in partnership with the local Sikh rice miller exporting rice bran to New Zealand. I would go every so often to the Battan Singh's house to eat some fiery goat curry wrapped in roti. It was delicious and was the beginning of my attachment to the use of capsaicin—the heating element in chillies.

Our Indian cookboy was a very good cook, and produced not only a variety of good Indian dishes but delicacies like devilled mudcrab meat, or delicate lamb brains *au gratin*. All of this I enjoyed with enthusiasm, but a further change came after another serious illness. This time it was a severe and life-threatening bout of dysentery which eventually left me skeleton-like. When the wretched cause of the infection was finally eliminated, and I started slowly to recover, the doctor advised building me up with plenty of milk, and said that my love of bananas should be encouraged. My Fijian friends educated me to find the best and the sweetest.

They said, 'forget about those big perfect-looking bananas we produce for the *kai vavalagi* (white folks), the really best ones have black spots on the skin—that's when you know the sugar has built up. But you have to get them at just the right time.' And I did. My appetite had been good, but now it was much keener and I learnt to be adventurous about food. I realised then, aged eleven, that eating was not merely about satisfying an appetite—taste and smell sensations were sensual delights which could provide an ever widening enjoyment. So, far from rejecting what one didn't know, I learnt that the richness of eating and drinking, as in the rest of my life, lay in variety. But that, I found, did not mean that one simply gorged on anything that came along. In testing the variety, one also sharpened one's discernment of quality.

Simple things could be marvellous. In the heat and the humidity of a tropical climate, there was nothing better than getting a drinking coconut just at the right moment—I had to get someone to climb the tree (I have never been able to manage it) when the juice was fresh with a light spritzig, the flesh had formed and just turned white and could be spooned out. No coconut taste is as lovely and delicate as that.

Apart from his poultry yard, my father had rented some land next door and had our garden boy grow vegetables there. I did not then take an interest in producing food. I was no gardener. I enjoyed eating some of the vegetables—we had snake beans, yams, eggplant (aubergine), bhindi (okra). Our cookboy baked dalo and kumara (sweet potato) in the oven in their jackets, or sliced the dalo and deep-fried it, and cooked eggplant in a variety of ways.

Another change in my life. At age thirteen I was sent back to South Australia to live with another aunt (this time an aunt by marriage) in Glenelg, by Adelaide's seaside and to go to school at St Peter's College. In the depression years, my Aunt had been Lady Mayoress of Adelaide for her widowed father the Lord Mayor, Sir Johnathon Cain, and she was still very much involved in charity and good works. The household was cared for, in those early years of the war, by two maids whose cooking, in my memory, was unremarkable. The best I can recall of my expanding interest in food was that on Sundays the maids disappeared, and my aunt usually made 'high tea'. She would produce a tray-mobile of foods just for us, to put together before the open wood fire—little meat pies, hot cocktail sausages, crumpets to be toasted over the coals and drenched in butter and honey, fresh scones with jam and cream.

As my dear friend Derek Nimmo would remark in that extraordinary voice, 'What Providence!' That, of course, was before the Japanese entered the war and life became more stringent. The maids disappeared to munitions factories and never came back. That was the end of domestic servants in Australia, except for the very rich. There was a whole change to social life. Food became frugal and there was rationing of most things. There was little room for good food or innovation. I had my first lessons in cookery because now, on occasion, I had to give my aunt a hand in preparing things.

The masters at school went off to the war and as a senior boy, I found myself running the school's scout troop. To go to camp, I had to see to the food and cooking, so I used my pocket money to buy my first cookbook. It was the *Commonsense Cookery Book* compiled by the New South Wales Public School Cookery Teachers' Association. So, I started cooking at scout camps to feed the young monsters. I didn't lose any scouts but I don't think they were entranced by my efforts.

Slowly a new world of interest in food opened for me. Cooking was fun and fascinating. You could concentrate and work out the process and produce something that was satisfying—if you gave it care and attention. And as I went on to university doing (among other studies) a history major, there was a new focus. Traditional history writers had tended to talk of dynasties, ambitions and power struggles. The Marxists, in correction, had pointed to neglect in historical analysis of class and economic interest but had neglected a driving force in trade and movements of population—food.

The history of mankind has been profoundly affected by the need for food and its refinements. In Greek and Roman times, in the Mediterranean and its surrounds, the provision of basic food supplies and the search for the flavours to enhance them has ensured wars, seated and unseated rulers and dynasties.

The invasion of the Roman Empire by the hordes of barbarians did not happen merely for loot but in search of better and surer bases and locations for food supply. The European discovery of the Americas was not merely in search of gold, but rather for an access to the spice trade essential to the post-barbarian food practice of Europe. How profoundly Europe and the rest of the world was affected by the use of food products from America. Only then did I discover how much of our present day foods have been in use generally in the world only since Columbus arrived on the shores of the Caribbean Islands. The basic starch of Ireland and the whole of the Slav world became the potato instead of the uncertain grain crops of the past. Italy was overtaken by the use of the tomato, Hungary by the capsicum. The list is enormous, for instance: chocolate, chillies, 'French' beans, pineapples, peanuts, allspice, turkeys, maize.

I started on what is a never-ending study of the history of food origins and uses and their effects on the daily lives and enjoyments of people in history, as well as on patterns of trade and movement of peoples and governments.

I started to learn the techniques of refined cooking—of concentrating flavour and ensuring tenderness of meats combined with contrasting textures. In Fiji I was befriended by the officer in charge of the experimental horticulture area of the Department of Agriculture, who took me to see their nursery and talk about the plants one could grow. His enthusiasm was contagious and I realised that my love could be enhanced by growing and caring for the food I cooked for my family and friends. I quickly grew to love getting my hands in the soil, talking to the plants and using produce from the garden with all its freshness and cooking it with care. I turned my attention to herbs as well. How vital they are to get great flavour!

In Fiji I started to grow bananas, taro, cassava and grenadillas. I couldn't, on a small domestic plot, produce the quantities the household needed—but it was a start, and in those days the markets were wonderful. Today they are much drearier and not nearly so well supplied. But then one could fill the back seat of the car for very little money with vegetables and fruits of great quality. Since my wife was laid up a good deal of the time with a difficult pregnancy, I essayed a lot of the cooking and found it both fun and relaxing. I was working hard as an advocate in the courts but I could escape from the stress by cooking and giving good food to my loved wife and to friends.

Back in Australia, we settled in Norwood and refurbished two old houses in succession. The second of these was an old vineyard house which had enormous cellars and still had hundred-year-old house vines. I once again met sultanas, muscatels and fruit trees—two plums, a nectarine and I added a fig. There was an area where I could start growing some vegetables. How good it was to get my hands into the soil and bring produce I had nurtured to the kitchen.

By now the children were starting to take some interest in food and I regularly cooked breakfast and most of the weekend meals. They pushed me to provide more variety in their breakfast dishes and I continued to explore those and hone my egg cookery—it is, after all, one of the bases of refined cooking. I learnt from Escoffier, whose republished work I bought as soon as it landed here, how to cook scrambled egg properly (he calls it the finest of egg dishes). And since, by then, I was the local member of Parliament as well as a busy barrister, I was pretty tired at night. But I gained relaxation and refreshment from studying the origins and history of food and their treatment as bedside reading before falling gratefully into exhausted sleep.

When I was a student, I had got to know a little about wine—my aunt and uncle used to have a sherry before dinner which I was invited to try, but at university college I had the occasional dry red or white and grew to appreciate how well wine and food went together. The culture of Adelaide then was very much a tea and beer drinking one, and those who drank wine in public were regarded with suspicion as 'winos'. There were wine bars, but they mostly sold fortified, sweet wines to seedy customers who came in for their 'fourpenny dark'. But I realised just how civilised it was to drink wine with one's meal, that food was enhanced by marrying the two tastes.

As I went round organising political campaigns, I was able to see and taste more of the wines of South Australia and this has led to a long and rewarding association. In Clare, in South Australia's mid-north, I searched for a winemaker who might be able to sell me some good claret in bulk, so that I could bottle and cellar it at home. The locals advised me to go to see 'Roly' Briks at his Wendauree vineyard. I explained to him what I wanted and he said, 'Aw yair. Come down here.'

We walked through his winery and from under a large cask he fished out a dusty bottle. He uncorked it, poured some into a glass and said, 'Have a suck of that and see what you think.' I did, and said, 'That's wonderful. Could I have some of that?'

He said, 'Tell you what I'll do. Every vintage I'll send you down a five-gallon keg of red. You can bottle it off. Burn a little sulphur in the cask, which I'll send you, and you return the cask next year.'

I said, 'Done!' and for years my sons and I bottled off marvellous Wendauree wines and put them down the cellar—they used to cost two shillings and sixpence a bottle in those halcyon days. While Mr Briks has passed on, I am happy to say that I have always managed to get some Wendauree wine. Australians have steadily come to understand and appreciate wine with their food so that now one expects to have it at lunch and dinner and on social occasions.

Sadly, in 1972 my wife and I parted and I went to live in a little flat while I planned to build a house for myself. I did all the cooking and continued learning and experimenting. My younger son was with me for a weekend and brought home a friend of his, who had been thrown out of home by his parents after a furious row. 'Could he also stay the weekend?' I said yes—provided his parents knew where he was. He stayed and I set about cooking. I later had a note from his mother who said, 'My heart bled when I saw him go off down the footpath, for what I thought would probably be a weekend with the Salvation Army—but thought it would do him good. Little did I know he would find a haven in the Premier's flat and feast on pheasant in Calvados!'

At this time, I formed a friendship with the Chief Minister of Penang, Dr Lim Ching Yew, which led to a close association between our States.

There was an historic connection—Sir Francis Light was not only the founder of Penang, but the father of Colonel William Light, the founder and planner of Adelaide. While I had experienced Malaysian cuisine before, my introduction to the techniques of cooking used in that very 'fused' cuisine, with elements of native Malay, Arab, Indian, Chinese, with some influences from English, Dutch and Portuguese, came with this association. In George Town, Dr. Lim—also a devotee of food plant growing and passionate about expanding Penang's resources—introduced me to all aspects of this wonderfully rich food opportunity. It was supported with enthusiasm by his wife and later by others among food lovers in Penang.

I started experimenting when I got home—and, oh, the joys of all those new experiences of tastes and textures. Returning to Penang over the years, I established a pattern—while they were alive—of going to the 'Sisters'—hawker food sellers on MacAlister Road, for their char kway teow (fried rice noodles) at breakfast, or taking a beca to go to a back street where the best yum cha was served in seemingly rather squalid conditions. Scruffy old tables spread onto the street and tea slopped into your cup (with much spillage, Cantonese style) but in fact everything was clean, carefully prepared and delicious. Or I would go to another stall in a bigger street to have the best of roti canai—the thinnest of dough whirled in the air, then quickly cooked on a hot grill and filled with your choice of curry—the texture much better than the roti of my childhood.

There were so many lessons for the historian. In Penang, as in most of South-East Asia, not only ginger but galingale was widely used. Now, there is a flavour that, like coriander, England lost—as was the case with so many flavours historically used in European countries—to their modern day food culture. Coriander, a Mediterranean rather than an Asian herb, was grown in Britain during the four hundred years of Roman rule, but disappeared with the invasion of our barbarian forefathers, so that now it is usually referred to there as 'Chinese parsley' and Australians of British descent have rediscovered it through their love affair with Thai cooking. Galingale (Malay lengkuas and Indonesian galangal) related to ginger has a remarkably different rather peppery taste. It appears however in the 'Cury' that was served at the table of the English king, Richard II. I also found that the Malaysians like many Asians (the Thais, Indonesians and Filipinos, and in a different way the Japanese) still knew what the Romans did, that using fish stock and concentrated dried fish paste does not add a fish flavour to dishes but is the best of natural flavour enhancers. Unfortunately that flavour and technique, used constantly by the Romans, was lost to Europe in the middle ages. There was so much to learn and profit by. There was, of course, the cooking of the Nonyas—the descendants of Chinese who settled in Malaysia in the seventeenth century and inter-married, but developed a distinct culture and cooking of their own—Lee Kuan Yew's mother wrote a book about it.

By 1973, I had managed to find a vacant block of land in my district of Norwood, Adelaide. It had been like looking for hen's teeth. When I was making plans for my house, the elderly owners of the adjoining property pointed out that they had a piece of land fifty feet by thirty, behind mine, and asked if I would I like to buy it. They would cut it off their title and add it to mine. I bought it with gladness in my heart. I could at last have a good vegetable plot. I planned the house around my kitchen. I wanted the living area to be one big central room with an open kitchen at one end. My architect was very worried that this would mean that kitchen mess and smells would obtrude. I said, 'That's life—when my friends come here I am likely to be in the kitchen and I don't want to shut myself off or to have them wandering into the kitchen, getting in the way while I'm cooking. So we'll create an audience area on the other side of the island bench and they can sit there and talk to me while I'm cooking.'

I moved into the house in 1974, and it has been my loved haven ever since. I have fruit trees—pomegranate, mulberry, two olives, loquat, macadamia, cumquat, tahitian lime, makrut lime, navel orange, meyer and lisbon lemon, grapefruit, granny smith apple, two avocados, wiggins peach, two figs, apricot and vines—sultanas muscatels and concord grapes, passionfruit and choko. I have a flourishing herb garden (including galingale) and my vegetable garden produces much that is fresh and rewarding. When I write about this people say to me—you must have a very large block. Well no. It is slightly bigger than the average suburban block in the vicinity. It is simply intensely planted and cultivated. I don't have large areas of manicured lawn. And I have joy.

• • •

In 1973 my friends persuaded me that I should write a cookbook. My political associates were horrified—'Premiers don't write cookbooks,' they admonished. I have never taken much notice of silly stereotypes in behaviour—I wrote the book and it has remained one which out-sold all others I have subsequently written by far, and there is not a week that goes by without someone saying to me 'I use your cookbook'. In it I pointed out that from the point of view of food, Australia is the most fortunate country in the world. We can grow anything there is to grow. We have fertile land, not only in temperate and sub-tropical climates, but the largest tropical area of any nation except Brazil. Early on in the period of European settlement Australians learnt to transport food efficiently and keep it fresh. With our vast distances we had to. So, from the early period we were eating fresh tropical fruits in southern cities, as well as the cold and temperate climate fruits and vegetable we could grow there. Our cuisine has never been subject to the restrictions of supply and variety which have forced the ethnic cuisines of Europe and Asia into more confined moulds. Moreover, as the most successful multicultural country in the world, we have a wider range of cooking traditions and methods readily available than anywhere else. No wonder so-called fusion cooking—putting together the tastes and techniques of Europe and the Pacific rim—started here. In my cookbook, I wrote of stir-fry techniques—little known then in Australia, and the cover photograph showed me at the stove with a wok. Australia today is the only predominantly European country where it is standard to have a wok burner as part of the cooking top, and every butcher has in his window display meats prepared for stir-frying.

In the book I wrote of my pleasure in sharing good food—one can show your love of those close to you by growing, preparing serving and eating good food. I could have added that there are joys to be had in the intellectual exercise of discovering the history of the growing and preparation of food, of understanding its evolution and that is so much part of sharing one's enjoyment in life. There is still so much to learn and to experience. This has been, and is, a true love to me.

NICHOLAS JOSE

Love of the Place

*F*rom the verandah I look down the cliff to a beach that is a scroll of white paper unfurling to the far distance. It is a distance known, since I have walked it regularly for years, in different tides and seasons, yet it forgets me. The rocks record no footprints. The noisy pebbles return at once to silence. The sand wipes out all tracks within the cycle of a day. The place does not remember. But then, memories *are* the place.

A boy stands upright in the shallows. Side-on to my gaze with the sun behind him, he is little more than a black weapon-thrower, lean and unfeatured in the darkening, flattening afternoon light. A blade of bone, sinew and muscle defines his shape against the mother-of-pearl sea and fiery pink light over the promontory beyond. His harpoon extends like a craning neck above his shoulder. Alone, still he pursues his task, aware of me only in theory, as an element of his world, not much different from the Pacific gull that lobs out of a blue sky to feed on his school of fish. What I see is an absence, a dark knife-shape erect in the lapping near-silence of late afternoon. He is far enough away, absorbed. What I see, what moves me, is not him but a memory of twenty-five years ago, a boy on the beach at dusk, a holiday-maker, solitary inhabitant of my world, walking on grey sand, wading in flat light, diving under surfaces with a harpoon when there was the chance of a catch, flinging the spear recklessly at a fish in the shallows, missing them by not allowing for the refraction of light through water.

My contemporary, more or less. Timid, I never approached. I left him as untouched by my gaze, perhaps, as he was untouched by my presence. He had others with whom he met and played on the beach, although he seemed to prefer being alone. Or had no choice. He was scarcely touched, as I was, by the pain of my not knowing him.

Or not knowing myself. For his image is elusive across twenty-five years except as an image of myself, featureless, flop-haired, gangling, undefined, yet having the eyes to record an indelible image, and an obscure ache that would become a concealed scar.

Days snorkelling over rockpools, underwater reefs, reedy shelves, sandy bottoms. The fish I hunted were stripy bream or zebra fish, their black and white stripes rippling like the dark weed that grew across the pale floor. Or my own frightening shadow, taking me by surprise like a shark's when I forgot and the angle of the sun cast it down behind me, hooking my peripheral vision. Or swimming through a submarine dreamscape, weightless, careless, skinless almost, thinking a blurred strip of shadow on the bottom mine, I was jarred to awakening by a ray that stirred its real stinger from the disguise of cloudy sand. To exist in water, among unfocussed shadows, not sitting or standing, flying. To float on the surface, my back burning in sunlight, goggled face downwards, gliding above the element like a bird, observing but not of it. Or diving deep, only to turn and rise into light, breaking through like a tern that has taken its flapping silver prey, the salt oil taste of fish in the mouth …

Rainwater for drinking and washing was scarce in the house. Boys, shower together. Not too long in the shower, boys. The cubicle of frosted glass was bejewelled with droplets of spray and steamed-up from the hot shower. Two boys jostled for space under the water jet, giving and taking, lathered bodies rinsed on one side, soapy on the other. No touching. Young men sheathed in privacy and self-definition. Like the plastic bags toddlers put over their heads to suffocate themselves. Desire to touch, to violate, to be violated, and fear growing the greater with desire. Contained within the glass cubicle. Peering through a plane of glass, a wall of water and heat, with blurred underwater vision. The spearhead quivering, poised to smash the glass to smithereens. To jagged, jugular danger …

The boy flings back a worthless zebra fish, dimpling the sea. The spear gash oozes fish blood. With a shriek a seagull drops, two others squawking behind to contest the claim. Flesh pecked to bone in lively dancing quarrel as the boy turns his back. He disappears up the beach to darkness and home.

From this scene come countless deceiving images and constructions, since the sea is a perfect blank and empty measure of ourselves, maintaining no loyalty, no memory, no personal ties. Knows nothing of our nostalgia, our serpentine undertow. Makes no promises of the future. The sea provides, merely, convenient readings for bravado, impossibility, putrid romance. Why think the sea can transform us? Why make the sea take on the actualities we invent for ourselves, the delicate, detailed lymph-nodes of memory? Lies. The madonna girl with brushed-out blonde hair writes on her wall in black texta the laughable lines from Baudelaire. *Free man, how you adore the sea! The sea is your mirror.* The morning after a night of unsatisfactory love with a dumb selfish surfboard rider with a soft dick she writes in a more private journal: *With a crash I'll split the glass. Behind it stands one I must kiss, person of love or death, a person or a wraith, I fear what I shall find* (Keith Douglas). She is still standing after the glass has split a number of times. Until she gives the game away.

I cooked my first meal here. Or should I say, there? Twenty-five years ago. My first celebratory meal, in fact—a dish defined as different from ordinary food. It was spaghetti bolognese—a misnomer. A creation. I understood bolognese to be a dish made using dry spaghetti from a packet, boiled in water with sauce added separately, not the spaghetti snippets that come with sauce out of a tin. Romance. Italy. Complexities of sauce unknown. It was fried strips of salami and chopped onion, tomato paste and water, carrot rings, seasonings, drowned parsley, stewed up together for ten minutes over a hotplate and spooned onto noodles which every effort had sought to render *al dente*. Resistant. Biteable. We were drunk and silly on a flagon of red wine and ate the food down without noticing the pressure against teeth. It was a sign, a sacrament, that pointed like a blood-dripping finger the direction of a long journey, of unimagined commitment and convolution, into food. Not love, as then we believed was our destination.

For the love was perfect already. There. Or here. Then. Or now. Since. Ever. We had driven through stubbled territory to arrive, dust on our skin from the open car window, the day the death of the poet Auden was reported on the radio. We travelled down and across the peninsula to the other side, a wide serene bay, a beach washed clean for us, a house perched on the edge of a cliff, a site to deal the cards of a lifetime. Where

> *Love was made*
> *Then and there: so halcyoned ...*

whispered the dead poet in our ears, that 'Since' nothing would equal or tarnish.

What nonsense! Quarter-century of life held hostage by a day, a night, a hot painful, oily, and, in the event, indecently hasty act of penetration. Love that does not last, and cannot die. A private business taking hold in the space of contradictions, where words cannot grip. Love the escorting angel, long dreamed, who walks down streets and by shopfronts that have never conceived of such a visitation, each object and scene renamed in passing. Love the secret witness, the shared proof. Love who finds you, who touches you. So as to leave you, afterwards, wholly alone.

Round cove and headland, into cave and along pier, past farmhouse to solitary tree we walked, following the sand. Everywhere we left our presence, like a dustcloth, or the smear of mercury particles when a thermometer smashes. Memory like a stain. None of it seems to remember us any more. Yet the presence—coastline, seabirds, wind-bent trees, tumbled rocks, sea—stands, to me, for love itself.

The shore appears sliced from out at sea. Beach, cliff, steps, cliff top, white caravan under stunted pine, changing sheds—his and hers, a pair of ti-trees, white water tank on rusty stand, and the house. From the verandah, looking down, the scene stretches continuously. As between threads on a loom the boatman is caught in opposing tensions, whether to drift out deep or pull in.

The boy along the beach stands in pink dusk, his harpoon poised in the air. He aims at a sand-coloured mullet or its shadow. His task, his generation, his life, are his. Yet I possess for myself something else of him, as only I can, carried for a quarter-century, constructed as loss, or tragedy, the big words of art. I claim from him a myth of absence.

I sat with chilly feet on the dew-damp verandah above the milky-grey sea and I drank strong tea from a stained mug the morning after. I reached for poems, I remember. *I sing the Body Electric ...* Words. From which grow

LOVE OF THE PLACE

Vermeer, Mozart, Tristan, yearning, renunciation. Without which no language of feeling. No feeling in my language.

I turn away this time, because I want a longer journey, down the echoing corridor.

Ditching a real love, I create a pure and perfect loss. The sensations of a life are all imaginary in the end, as the erased sand reminds, and the unmindful rocks, and the inky sea that no ink can inscribe.

Fisherman are out. One fisherman to a boat, until the last shreds of light, reluctant to join the company on shore, or the different loneliness of an empty dwelling and a cold bed. Pelicans fly in twos in the wake of a porpoise that dips and disappears. One. No, two, partnering each other in a porpoise *pas de deux*. Slowly the fisherman come in, checking their pots on the way. A violet sky is pocked with stars as the moon's presence intensifies. Current flow against the wind makes silver ribs in the sea. It becomes dark enough to imagine anything, while light enough to fancy forms and movements, stories continuing in layers. The boy with the harpoon returns, a black shape. He wades out. The shoreline is like a white frill of fat on raw dark meat. He continues, deeper into the water. The sea. Rippling, wind-scalloped, tide-sucked, black and silver weave of utmost complexity ...

He dives, down like an arrow. The lone swimmer is in darkness. Like a knife his body cuts the mesh of the sea as if he is tearing cloth—

> *How, but with some real focus*
> *of desolation*
> *could I, by analogy,*
> *Imagine a love ...?*
>
> W. H. Auden, *Amor Loci*

Emma Tom

Rays

Something about the way she's lying there drives me crazy. Not good crazy. Not sexed-up, who-wants-ya-baby crazy.

Hazy crazy.

She's a pretty girl standing upright but flapping round on her back with black hair through her mouth and the weight of her face giving her extra gills makes her look like something unspeakable unearthed from the ocean.

Wendy Warner croaks my name then, spasming and thrashing about like a fish in a bucket.

Hey, mullet girl, I want to say. How about I batter you in beer and serve you up on a gold-cornered plate with a crack the size of an earthquake? How would you like that, eh?

Outside the window above the steel bed the freeway traffic light changes from green to red as someone crash dominos another line of motorbikes down the long hill. Above the lights is a skyscraper with a digital weather readout and a blank advertising billboard.

YOUR LOGO HERE, it reads in neon, the third O stuttering insanely.

According to this building, it is 7°C.

12.01 am.

7°C.

Who is she anyway, this fish in my bed causing the cold?

Don't ask me.

Wendy Warner's identity is causing nothing but trouble.

Only the morning before I tell a man I have never met on one end of a number full of nines that the scaly creature swimming in leather beside me requires a taxi.

'Passenger's name?' he bleats through the gaping black doughnut of the telephone. 'PASSENGER'S NAME?'

But for an endless second I cannot recall who she is and have no choice but to shout my own name before the fish catches on and blends me into a smooth filth down in the salty lair.

Goodbye WENDY WARNER, I call with unnecessary force from the front door as she runs towards the taxi's hoot (imagining this will make it more than clear that all is well).

But Wendy glares over her shoulder and in the confusion I panic, convinced her long left leg will be caught in the car door and grated along the freeway like a terrible torn ribbon of evening dress.

Outside the window above the bed, the traffic light changes again. Green, orange and red in an endless stop and start.

Overhead in the roof is a plaster fault that runs from one corner of the ceiling to the next.

Due south, the fingers of Wendy Warner spray across fine, white cheeks bleeding electrical light.

She opens her eyes, then. Turns those loose, grey sockets straight onto me.

'Roll over, Ray,' I say to escape the look.

Then freeze, shocked at what I have said.

Next to me in the bed Wendy is completely still. She does not roll as I have requested but neither does she ask why I have called her Ray. In fact if I didn't know better I'd say she slept through the entire disaster.

I am stunned.

Mortified.

Utterly unhinged.

There is no choice but to count consonants and chain smoke until dawn, convinced as I am that if I slow down for a second it could happen and I could call her Ray again.

When I wake, Wendy is in the kitchen frying bacon that smells like lavatories.

This girl is trying to kill me, I think in a poisonous daze.

I sleep again and dream I buy her a black and white dog with a three hundred and fifty dollar price tag stapled to its ear. But the dog turns out to be blind and walks backwards into a lake of wet bitumen on a new freeway full of flashing traffic lights and falling motorbikes and there's nothing anyone can do.

When I wake for the second time she's back in bed, hair sliding over my face as she flips the pages of a magazine she's read a hundred times before. It's Wendy's fantasy to see her cheeks on these pages. And as I reach out to pinch the glaring dreamer, it almost happens again.

My lips are apart. The name is up and running into the top half of my neck and I have little choice but to employ the old open-fist-down-the-throat trick to hold it back.

Wendy turns to look with her eyes sharp and her mouth straight. She wants to know why I have my hand in my mouth, but what can I say?

'Christ, Ray!' (Is the hideous whisper I'd nominate.) 'What the hell are you doing to me, mullethead?'

Instead I spit out the fist, finger at a time, and put my teeth to hers. It does the trick and for a while the only sound is the wet gurgle of our throats.

The straight-mouthed look I have exterminated is not a natural expression, anyhow. Left to their own devices, Wendy Warner's jelly eyes wobble and her mouth explodes in every which direction. Really comes into its own, as she'd say herself. But someone once told Wendy this straight-eyed style of staring was 'inscrutable' and she thought that was altogether a good thing. The fish adopts the inscrutable gaze many times a day and each time I know exactly what it means. It means she's wondering how long it will before I do something evil to her again.

Like call her Ray.

In the empty, blue light of the winter air I crunch rows of letters into fresh paper on the typewriter at my desk while Wendy considers more of last century's magazines. The afternoon turns into later afternoon and eventually there are no more excuses not to speak to her. Even banging away on the toilet with the old Olivetti see-sawing across my knees doesn't keep her away.

'What are you thinking?' she asks, dressed in clothes from my cupboard with dangling sleeves clutching at straws past her fingers.

'Getting an injection in your eye,' I answer, banging away at my lap.

Wendy narrows her eyes and straightens her mouth.

'Followed by getting an injection in your mouth or some other part of your head,' I add (thinking all the while, 'stick that in your pipe and smoke it, Ray!').

If I was in a game show, the wrong answer buzzer would be shrieking and my pupils would be the size of pinheads.

News of my latest phobia is not what Wendy wants to know.

'Poppet?' I say.

'Yes?' she says.

'Can't a person get a little privacy in their own goddamn bathroom?'

Bang bang bang.

176 consonants.

69 vowels.

Fairly standard for work performed under these less-than-ideal conditions.

Wendy asks me What? (Stands for WHAT? WHAT ARE YOU THINKING?) another eight times before the day is over.

'Having someone make a mistake when they're giving you an injection,' I tell her.

Then: 'Watching an injection on television.'

And five more answers all the way down to injecting fruit.

My unfortunate replies are drawn directly from a desensitisation list offered as a cure for needle phobia. This and other advice was provided to me by a professional head sweeper on the tacit understanding that when she charged me a hundred and seventy dollars an hour, I would pay her.

'You are disassociated,' she told me after ignoring a referral from the family doctor that described me as a pleasant person with little or no agoraphobic symptoms. 'Your syndrome is one of depersonalisation.'

'Depersonal!' I yapped. 'Depersonal! You try living beneath Your Logo Here and see how you like it!'

Lying to Wendy about what I am thinking is hardly optimal behaviour but there is no way I can tell her the truth—that I have to remain on guard and on alert to prevent the name slipping out again.

After all, then Wendy would undoubtedly ask: Why Are You Calling Me Ray?

And I would have to tell her: Well, My Glistening Little Sharkling, I Have No Goddamn Idea.

Lying to Wendy is hardly optimal behaviour but neither is outstaying your welcome. I wait for her to leave but she simply turns her underwear inside out and remains.

Fortunately she evicts herself before I wake. This is because the offices of Noble Beverages in the high rise overhead anticipate the pleasure of her company at 7:00 a.m.

It is, however, only a matter of hours before I am woken by the phone.

'Baltic Services,' I say in a language designed to confuse, 'Young Murat speaking.'

'I know it's you,' says Wendy.

'Why, hello there, Wendy Warner,' I say with special emphasis on my remembrance of her name. I look up at YOUR LOGO HERE and note that it is 16°C and 10:08 a.m.

'How are the fine folk at Noble Beverages treating you up there today?'

'We've run out of creamified soap again,' she says. 'The nozzle on the machine is clogged.' And then as an afterthought: 'I can see into your kitchen from the storeroom, you know.'

And there is a long and exacting silence.

'Why did you ring me?' I say finally. 'To tell me you had nothing to say to me?'

Silence.

'Sorry!' I bark. 'That's why I ring you, of course! Obviously I am highly disoriented.'

'Actually,' Wendy says. 'I do have something to say.'

'Mmm hmm?'

'Last night when I was lying in bed watching the moon I was thinking "I've really fallen, I've really fallen for you".'

'Ah yes,' I answer in lieu of sense. 'That meddling moon.'

But Wendy cuts me off.

'You were sleeping,' she continues (as if that explains everything). 'And I was thinking that even though I'd fallen for you before, I must have hit something on the way down.'

'Down,' I parrot mindlessly, dreaming of phone arson.

'Exactly,' she says. 'But whatever it was, whatever sort of ledge it was I hit, I realised yesterday that it had detached or broken off somehow, and I was falling for you more.'

'Falling …'

'Don't you understand what I'm saying?' she snaps. 'This is it for me. This is the one.'

I end our call with the excuse of allergy, but in truth it's all I can do not to call her Ray.

At some stage in the future, Wendy Warner and I meet to eat spaghetti with fish in an underlit cafe on an overlit road. I blame myself, even before the fight starts. But something about the way she starts in with the scrutable inscrutable business drives me crazy.

Not amaze-me crazy. Not owner-operated, give-it-to-me-lazy crazy.

Hazy crazy.

'You're drunk,' she says.

It's true, but I have no choice but to demonstrate the reverse.

'No, I'm not,' I answer. 'And I can name cars to prove it.'

'Barton Commander CXI,' I say, banging the glass of the restaurant window with my fork. 'Panda Reliant. Amor Fuego GTX. Rogets 404. Colonial Trans-Zip 82 model.'

Each time a car passes and my eating utensil connects with glass, the two pretty men at the table next door watch our jabbering reflections, wondering why Wendy Warner and I can't make a little less noise.

'Nylon Budgie LX,' I announce. 'Vox 1600. Stanza Marillion with different badges. Oh, and the inimitable Spatch Moxie. Torquey little bitch that one.'

The last taxi I fork pulls up outside the restaurant and releases a woman with patches of hair missing and fake leopard skin leggings. Directly in front of her, a dwarf in a wheelchair pounds his way down an alley the colour of panthers.

'You said you'd be nice to me tonight,' Wendy sniffs nicely.

I hadn't, of course, but she's almost right. I had *intended* to be nice, even though I hadn't told her so.

To celebrate three days of not calling her Ray.

As it turns out, my intentions make no difference whatsoever. Within two hours we're home and she's sitting on the undecided side of the bed, stockings in one hand, screaming.

'Well, do you? Do you want me to leave? Yes. Or. No?'

'Stop breathing like that,' I say, having the drunken revelation that if we could only drag race to work this out then things would greatly improve. 'You'll hyperventilate.'

Wendy locks herself in the front seat of her car beneath the tea-less offices of Noble Beverages. There's no sound but I know she's out there, twisting her hair into corkscrews and panting over the fluffy steering wheel.

2:18 a.m.

1°C.

Unseasonably chaotic.

Half an hour later she returns. 'Well should I?' she says unnecessarily. 'Should I just go?'

And as she cries and clutches at my face, the room seems to fold in on itself. Wendy's like the plumbing, I think. I hate the idea of the stuff but can't seem to get by without it.

'You're impossible,' she howls. 'You're a nightmare. You can't even say whether you want me here or not.'

'Well,' I tell her, my mind in agonising cramps. 'I guess that's up to you. I guess that's up to you, Ray.'

When I wake the next morning I can't remember going to sleep. Can't remember whether we're still fighting or, for one torn moment, whether six comes before or after seven.

Bits and pieces of memory dodge like flash cards behind my eyes but there is no big picture. And the bed is a brothel. Torn corners. A cruentous slime across the sheets. And no sign of Wendy.

I wonder in a blackly comic fashion whether I have taken her life. But fish-o-cide seems out of character, even for me.

No-one is on hand to confirm or deny. I should be more concerned, make a phone call, send something via courier. But the most I can muster is a choked grunt.

'The key to all this,' I say aloud, 'seems to be Ray.'

It could be minutes or maybe days of hard thinking before an animal barks faintly from the past and I begin remembering Rays.

And strangely enough, as it turns out the question is not so much who? as which?

The first is many decades ago. I am much shorter then, a child reading on someone's bed with the sky outside a slick sick orange because it is late in the day and raining. Water slips down the outside of everything, assembling jewels against the glass and signalling—in my mind at least—imminent extraterrestrial invasion.

Ray is a dog. An overhaired, leonine scavenger with cartoon habits and a black and white mouth that never shuts. And as I lie there reading it licks my hand with its soft tongue. Licks around the fleshy part of my child's forearm and the knob of my elbow and the spotty curve of my shoulder. Licks at my face and runs its thin tongue over the corner of my eyes.

And as I slip my lips apart to shout at the wet window aliens, Ray the dog licks inside my mouth and tastes the underside of my cheeks and suddenly my hands are where they shouldn't be and in the deepest part of my stomach is an airy feeling as big as a spaceship.

That night, when I am eating dinner at the table with the parents, the dog slouches under the table and licks my knee and I shout, 'Piss off, Ray. Get outside.'

The others applaud me for my shouting.

'That fucking bludger,' says one of them—presumably my father. 'That fucking Ray is a damn bludger.'

The second Ray I remember is a short-distance sprinter not a dog. A singlet-wearer from school with dull ping pongs for peepers and arms always jammed out at his side like a Hills Hoist.

'They make me want to hang out my clothes,' I tell Raymond after the others go inside and it is only me and him left on the cold grass outside the farm. 'Those stick-out arms of yours.'

'Don't get weird on me,' he says, folding his arms in against his side. 'And move your arse over here, will you?'

But I stay where I am, pressing my knees to my chest and feeling my pulse running with heavy boots through my wrists.

'Did I tell you I once witnessed the alien invasion?' I say, even though by now I know it was only rain on glass.

'Did I tell you I've wondered what it would be like to do it with everyone in the grade?' he replies. 'I've decided that after Lo Watson you'd be the best.'

This, of course, surprises me greatly. Only that day I have been speaking to my father.

'Am I still too big?' I ask.

'Well,' he says after some thought, 'when you sit in the bath does the lard around your belly still gather like carpet rolls?'

'Yes,' I answer.

'Then you might as well run everywhere carrying two sacks of potatoes over your shoulder.'

My father gives me the 'oversized load' sign to wear around the house as a reminder and then goes away and returns with three rolls of his own. They are not carpet rolls. They are map-sized sheets of shiny paper spiralled into sticks.

'I thought you should have a look at these,' he says. 'What do you think?'

But when I unravel the vast photographs, I don't know what to say at the pictures of the naked people climbing each other from every direction.

I think of these photographs as Ray the short-distance runner moves close and touches me with both big hands. I look up and notice how in some places the sky is threadbare and unravelling, missing stars. Aliens, perhaps. Breaking and entering the galaxy.

I keep my back as straight as possible so Ray won't notice too much lard. My father made me leave the house with the 'oversized load' sign but it is now spirited down the side of my jeans.

There is the shriek of a ripped stitch as Ray presses his thin lips against my dry ones and flaps his tongue in and out of my mouth. Our teeth crack together and he pushes me onto the ground, rolling around on top of me like a wolf in an old corpse.

'So this is climbing,' I think. 'I see.'

One week later, I go to his house with everyone else to watch videos and there he is, laughing more than anyone in a white singlet with wiry straps.

In the first film a woman with red cheeks is knocked unconscious and two men in overalls bring her back to life by climbing her. I recognise one from my father's photographs and then notice Ray has gone.

Eventually I unearth him in a room off another room at the back of the house with a blond high jumper between his knees.

'Ray?' I ask with my eyes from the doorway.

'Forget it,' he hisses like someone out of a film. 'It'll never work. I want someone what's really horny.'

Raymond the Runner, I think in the present tense. You had the sharpest teeth and the heaviest legs of almost any Ray I have ever known.

The third Ray is actually a Raylene. Raylene the Dentist, in fact. She appears many years later, around the time I commence hypnotherapy to relieve myself of certain unpleasant recollections of my father's funeral.

The hypnotist is a watch waggler with soft grey hair and too many blue cushions.

'Imagine a safe place,' she tells me after counting backwards in twos. 'Imagine a safe place where you can watch the film of you.'

But all I can think of are my father's rolls and an alien stick child with a head three times the size it should be.

Outside the clinic the sky is a dull red and I suddenly realise that since I have been visiting the hypnotherapist, my wrists have been shrinking. Either that or everything else is enlarging.

Stunned, I stare down at the silver watch that now sags in evil metallic loops from my arm, catching on everything I pass.

'Watch it,' the red-headed dentist yodels as it plucks a woollen thread from her black overwear and stretches it into a high wire between us.

'My apologies,' I mime into a tin can on my end of the string. 'With wrist shrinkage, a certain degree of watch sagging is only natural. But this taking of hostages is beyond the pale!'

Raylene thinks little of my excuses—we are joined by a single woollen thread outside a clinic for the buffing of dentures, after all. But the way her pale eyebrows arch away from those green cat eyes of hers (as if there has been some terrible falling out between them) has me under a spell.

'The film of you will have boundaries,' the hypnotherapist has already explained. 'You can change the scenes whenever you want to.'

'All right,' I tell Raylene. 'Cut to interior shot. Lilac Spraddler's Eatery. The booth furthest from the curtain. You and I over yellow curry and black tea.'

Raylene stares deeply from beneath that fighting forehead of hers.

'My treat,' I add, to assure her of what I am suddenly convinced is my unshakable generosity. 'On account of the jumper.'

For two weeks after that first curry I can think of nothing except Raylene. Then, for a further two weeks after that, nothing except for Raylene thinking nothing of me.

A month passes, and all I get from her is a referral to a practitioner of natural medicine who covers my toes with pins and my back with bottles of boiling air.

'I think I love you,' I tell her via the mail. My toes leak and the bruises across my back have turned the colour of prune slops but I have thought of her so supremely these past four weeks that I am turned inside out. Like an inverted bed jacket with all the seams and labels exposed to the evening.

'Sorry,' she says via phone call on receipt of my confessions. 'But it's just not possible. I'm very busy, you see.' As if all I have asked for is a free polish and extraction.

The night after that there is a note under my windscreen wiper. 'Thanks for your company,' it reads. 'You're a special person. Luv Ray. Cross cross cross cross.' And a week later she invites me back to her farm under the pretence of avocado difficulties.

Her wooden home is on the side of a steep descent. Three young relatives live in rooms off the balcony but on this particular night they are dancing many kilometres north in a hall with wooden floors so springy a good two-thirds will return home concussed.

In the fading light, Raylene's hair is the colour of grass fires. 'It's getting late,' she says before the sun has even half set. 'Only a fool would drive now. You'd better stay.' And her belly shakes like a beautiful, half-set dessert.

The next morning I find Ray in the kitchen swallowing whole eggs with the three others. No place has been set for me at the table, there is not even a chair, and for a full nauseous minute I stand, watching them eat.

Eventually Ray looks up, a vile brick of toast caught in one corner of her mouth. 'Oh hello you,' she says, looking me straight in the face. 'If you'd said you were coming over today I could have made you some breakfast.'

Outside, I grab hold of the forgetful dentist's arm.

'Ray,' I say. Then forget what I am going to say.

She is so short with me she practically sinks from view.

'If you'd *said* you were coming over today I could have made *arrangements*,' she says, clearing each word as if it is a sentence unto itself. 'As it is I must run.'

And so it continues, week after week. Raylene inviting me over, pointing out that it is unsafe to drive and then forgetting me the next day.

After many such months of concern for my road safety, one morning she announces that if I do not stop arriving unannounced in the a.m. she will alert the appropriate authorities.

And after that I descend into a deep concrete pit for a good five years.

Curled like a question mark in the disfigured bed with still no sign of Wendy, I force myself to keep concentrating, to continue remembering. But to the best of my recollections there are no Rays of any description until Raymond DeMexico.

DeMexico, as you have no doubt read, made a pretty fortune speculating on the relative values of non-precious ores and minerals against each other in the decades of excess. But my own joint enterprises with the millionaire balloonist are hardly considered fit for exposure in the public arena.

Six months I spend in underling employment in the largest of the six skyscrapers bearing DeMexico's name before the great man and I finally meet.

I don't remember exactly why I am stretched beneath my workstation examining bite marks beneath my desk on the day of his tour. Yes I do. I am suffering from what I suspect to be defervescing plague and am nursing a spidery headache. As I retreat from the mindless hum of the office to lie staring up at the flaking yellow wood beneath my desk, it drives me crazy, drives me to distraction to think that in all the months I have worked at this desk I never noticed these pale splinters beneath the surface.

DeMexico's group moves from the executive lifts towards my end of the office at the very moment I let my head fall back to the squares of carpet searching for further signs of furniture betrayal. Things certainly look different from down here and it strikes me that maybe this isn't my table. Maybe this isn't my desk. Maybe this isn't even me.

'Which shoes was I wearing the day I started?' I demand of the underside.

And then, right at the moment Raymond DeMexico's enormous laced shoes park themselves behind my swivelling chair, I notice the bite marks. Bite marks all over the legs of my desk.

'Help!' I yelp, more at the thought of the great fangs that left these indents than DeMexico's tap on my shoulder.

But of course when I pass out the great man blames himself and when I wake I am lying beneath his desk in an office the size of a sharkarium.

'I hope you'll forgive me for installing you so close to the waste paper receptacle,' he says on his knees, running a hand through that thick short hair, that sly crutch of a chest. 'But I thought you might be more comfortable down there.'

And something about the way he grovels before me drives me crazy.

Not erase-me crazy. Not state banquet, let-me-have-it stagey crazy.

Hazy crazy.

And so it begins.

The whole time we are together I never know how much is biblical and how much is artistic. There's no doubt that pants-down plays a part. But the fascination I have with altering DeMexico is aesthetic. I was never one for art in my youth, but sometimes the masterpieces I leave in his skin impress even me.

Sometimes I use implements, sometimes my hands, sometimes only my free will.

Either way, there is no escaping the fact that Ray DeMexico's wife has almond eyes and mid-length chestnut hair with natural copper highlights. I know this because I have observed her face in the Karl of Switzerland hair curling television advertisement on at least twelve occasions.

Often I ask how can she not realise, what with the open canvas and closed frame he has become. But he just says that (what with their mutual interests in the endangered tiger shrew) he can't recall the last time they patronised the arts.

I am content with this partnership until DeMexico becomes messy, careless of who sees us where and doing what, and in an instant the great man becomes moth-like to me.

One night after he rises to clean himself up, I roll and find myself sticking to a cordial spot on the edge of the bed. I look closely at the sheets but see nothing. Roll again and collapse straight into another transparent swamp. I turn on the light and see nothing but white linen, all the while my hands sticking on and off to the thick pools of invisible grease.

Shortly afterwards I announce I shall be seeking alternative employment.

Raymond doesn't give in easy. He continues arriving at my house unannounced and turning up on the end of my telephone at all sorts of odd hours until eventually I phone his wife at the family home.

'Rachel,' I say when she picks up the phone. 'I may not know much about art but I know what I don't like and that's your DeMexico. Please have him removed from my gallery at once.'

I'm sure I don't have to tell you of the unpleasantness that follows, although I for one would have thought the popular press had better things to do with their hands than fondle the mindless wars of the DeMexicos and their expensive menageries. Suffice to say that if Ray DeMexico ever resurfaces in this city again the financial market regulators and the RSPCA will have a field day.

Back in real time, I try hard to remember if there are other Rays I have forgotten or overlooked. Other places and faces make themselves known to me but I am fairly certain I have covered the major players.

Darkness arrives again and as it does I realise YOUR LOGO HERE has been replaced by the unmistakable 'half-full or half-empty?' reservoir mascot of Noble Beverages. I feel strangely peaceful and wonder if the free falling Wendy will find it in herself to return.

But it turns out she has never left. Just as I take note of the time and temperature (7:52 p.m., 12°C, predictably chilly) Wendy walks into the room with her hair wet and smelling of soap. She hasn't scrubbed up well but at least she looks better than when she's flat on her back beneath the traffic lights.

'Your logo's here,' I say, laughing aloud at the thought of it.

'What?' she says,

'Noble Beverages,' I say pointing up at the new sign on the towering advertising building. 'Not that it makes a lick of difference!' (Depersonalised deschmersonalised.)

I pat the bed beside me and Wendy sits, her eyes huge and red and her cheeks warm in my hands.

'You know,' I say with mock seriousness. 'You *are* the only one. You're all I've ever known. Maybe we'll even be together forever.'

Wendy Warner's eyes grow wider than ever as deep inside I shake at the hilarity of it all

'Oh,' I add, 'and Ray?'

The black-haired girl looks up.

'Roll over, would you, Ray?'

And she does.

ADIB KHAN

Between Eros and Agape

Why do I recall herbs? Parsley ... rosemary. Sage and thyme. Unrelated words, and yet their collective association invokes strong sensations. Meanings and feelings. Something intense and personal. A belated discovery that cannot be shared ... Who are all these noisy people? Stalls, merry-go-rounds and ferris wheels. Shrieks of delighted children. Fluttering awnings and a whirl of colours. The silhouette of a traveller with a message at a fair. *Remember me to one who* ... There was a song. Fragments of memory drift by like debris in the dark hollowness of space. If there is a present, it is motionless. Dying without a fuss.

Now that I wish to say what you quietly longed to hear in the grey landscape of my creation, there is no voice to reach. Is there any point in cluttering up these vast spaces of blankness with doctors, bedpans, tubes and gadgets? I can be no more than a puppet strung on the slender threads of memory. Regrets whirl around me, feeding like sharks on chunks of remembrance. An imperfect world becomes visible through the mesh of restless emotions.

But here? There are no days, afternoons or nights. I am the sole inhabitant of a barren land under the permanence of an inert sky. For company I have the litter of my thoughtless years. Self-concern ... obsessions ... my desires. The unheeded warning of an old story. Leiriope wasn't my mother, and yet I was condemned to gaze into the pool of treacherous possibilities and discover self-love. I walk among feelings and ruptured memories.

The arsenal of lies is almost exhausted. In the sterility of the room there can be no revival. I know ... Can you come with me? There I go again ... As if it were possible! I have clawed and hammered the walls. The caul is unbreachable. Only sounds filter through. I can hear you ... oh, and Judy ... my parents. Your mother too. Her voice is raspy and disapproving. Are her hands eager to turn off the switches? Has she spoken to you about the satisfaction of revenge? Perhaps I imagine too much. Couldn't you bring Judy more often? Voices of strangers—polite and comforting, intended to induce hope.

Fear is drifting in the silence of an unending mist ...

And when you finally kneel to console yourself in the seclusion of an empty chapel, how will you remember me? Mumbled words, interrupted by pale images of the early years. I shall try to reach you. Of course you understand that I cannot promise to succeed when all others have been unable to penetrate the awesome silence. Perhaps my departure will be an eloquent apology. An absence that will ring in your ears. Echoes of those carelessly uttered words that have lain dormant since the days of extravagant planning. *Future ... Forever ...* A life without ripples. Undying love riding on the back of untenable dreams ...

I am tired of roaming this wilderness without destination. Will I meet the wandering Jew? I am thirsty. Ah, you could always read my intentions ...

I see the shadows rising from your mind ... Isn't that what you said as we lay on the mat of wild grass? The caramel light of summer draped itself on the lateness of a still afternoon. The strawberries were sweet–ripe, almost a bruised maroon. I hesitated. They reminded me of death—a smudge of coagulated blood in the whirlpool of rainbow colours. A minor blemish in the clarity of an expansive horizon.

They are perfect just before they begin to decay ... Restless devils whirled in those eyes. I thought about the currents of life that rippled under the winter whiteness of your dress. My head spun pleasantly after the excess of that second bottle. Then you hummed and sang that song. Slowly. The words were tinged with melancholy. Were you thinking of mortality in the haze of that endless afternoon?

Are you sad?

The question startled you. *No ... Yes! Yes, I am mourning the inevitable passing of a moment's perfection.*

Your arms were spread like extended wings. We drifted in a pale light above pools of murmuring water, rising above the hills to pass the sun-kissed clouds, pausing to listen to the harp of an idyllic future. Even the magnitude of the sky did not astonish us. The dreams of conquest were all so believable. Somewhere, between the vision of the afternoon and the blindness of twilight, there were promises and decisions. The sap continued to flow, even when the brief journey ended.

It is strange how I should now think so often about that day we measured ourselves to fit into the predictability of a tailored life. How plausible the words sounded.

Another interruption? The voice is polite. Controlled and reassuring. Like a warm wave lapping over a body immersed in water.

... *No change, Mrs Laker. He is not in any pain. There is every reason to be encouraged by his stable condition* ... A young man stamping his lies on the world, attempting to be professional.

How stubbornly the shards of memory cling to the submerged crevices and dark corners, unwilling to emerge. Like shy, veiled brides in some foreign culture. Why are the hills so brown and empty? Should I wait for a white horse to gallop across the barren slope? Listen. The wind strums the emptiness of a life drained of its achievements. Ashen-coloured remembrance and the whispers of elusive apparitions. Do I smell lilacs in a crystal bowl of cold water?

I am the rose of Sharon and the lily of the valleys ...

Did I make a sound just then? A twitch of the hand perhaps? Was that an exclamation of hope and surprise?

A familiar landscape emerges again, full of sound and old secrets ...

As we napped, exhausted by the possibilities of unruly laughter and outrageous flirtation, the clouds moved in like the billowy cloaks of ancient sky gods. When the rain came, we didn't run. Under a tree you read to me from a slim volume of poetry. Were they promises I was meant to keep? Such extravagant words! They belonged to an age of selfless devotion. Did they understand true love then? I remember ...

And I will make thee beds of roses
And a thousand fragrant posies
A cap of flowers, and a kirtle
Embroidered all with leaves of myrtle ...

A quivering ray of the uncertain sun touched your naked arm. We straightened the stooping day with the strength of whispered deceptions. Ah, how warm it was in the enclosure of your strawberry mouth. Peace fought with passion. What is love but God's gift that is sometimes packaged by the devil? The mirage of love—a display of endless tomorrows and vows of illusion.

Come live with me and be my love ...

I wasn't wise enough to look around the corners of that veiled invitation.

Must you leave now? I cannot feel the touch of your hands. Did you stroke my forehead just then?

I will see you tomorrow, love ...

Is it out of habit that you speak, or do you believe that your voice can reach me like the sound of a foghorn on a quiet waterway? How far away is tomorrow? Does it lie somewhere in the darkness that is carved inside me?

Don't worry, Mrs Laker. We will monitor him throughout the night. Get some rest. Good night.

Footfalls. I am stranded on the shore of a calm sea, a reluctant witness to your departure. The immensity of the night accentuates my loneliness. Oars dip into the water. The boat glides noiselessly into the dark. Will you return as Charon to take me to the other side? Oh, the stars are cold ...

How often did I perceive your anguish with less than genuine concern? Yes, there were blips of guilt. More than I cared to admit. Regret stretches tightly across the bubbles of remembrance. I cannot say if it was a passing fancy or a need to steady my faltering steps. I rushed through the thirties, grabbing life by the fistfuls as the years gathered momentum. The fulfilment of wayward passion ... Is that your mother intruding? *Lust*! she snorts ... is a transitory diversion between the panic of mortality and the resentment of boredom. It wasn't always like that. Once there was dew sprinkled freshness in the life we charted ...

And how seriously I listened to the priest and murmured dutifully, *I will ... I do.* Simple, wonderful man! His structure of the universe in place, dangling the certainty of contentment for us to pluck. There was such serenity of order in the chapel, as though life itself had been purged of everything unpredictable and chaotic. Beaming faces. Noble words spoken with the fervour of an unwavering conviction. A straight path. Signposts everywhere. The imperatives of marriage sounded so easy to follow. Nothing said about rust or decay, changes and growth ... the dullness ... the dangers of meltdown.

I hear the robust voice. *What therefore God has joined together, let no man put asunder ... St Paul teaches that the husband must love his wife as Christ loved the Church* ... Ad nauseum ... Torrential flow. At that point your father had a coughing fit. He died the next week. Poor man! Perhaps the religious fumes were too much for him. *In the joys and sorrows of life, in prosperity and adversity, they share their companionship, faithfulness, and strength* ... How often we accept words without grasping their long-term implications. I was not blessed with the wisdom of Tiresias. Why is it that only in suffering we stand close to the cold, bleak peak of wisdom? And then too it sometimes rains dust and memories on a parched land.

The beach was perfect that summer. It didn't seem possible that the week could ever end. Everything slowed to a luxurious crawl. We were greedy for life. The voracious appetite of the young. Who could possibly believe that Destiny could sometimes display a dark hand? We created a shimmering future and hung it on the peg of an afternoon's rainbow. Dissatisfaction ... boredom ... unhappiness. The plagues of lesser mortals. We were gifted with wings to rise above the pitfalls of human experiences. Under the stars, everything was possible. The lies were sincere and whispered with a fierce commitment. We were the prophets of our own future. What could the sea possibly know? The crashing waves were merely jealous. Wasn't it true that the sun always chased away the storm clouds?

There are moments in our lives when we search for Arcadian perfection and live with the conviction of fairytale endings. The nymph and the youth rest in the orchard, drunk on the nectar of self-deception. The bounty from the tree of life was to be our entire world—illuminated and full of astonishing significance. Even Jason's quest was not gilded with dreams of such riches. Were we careless? Could we have prevented a drought? Lazy caretakers perhaps. The leaves drooped, yellowed and curled. Naked branches—withered and died.

I do not know when the weariness set in. How does one guard love? I was too busy scrambling up the rungs of prosperity, kicking and swinging, striving for the peak. Nothing unfair about it. From the top of the heap one can gaze at heaven. I read *Leviathan* and *The Prince* at university. The Englishman and the Italian knew about the desperation of ambition and the hunger of greed. Nothing bloody or violent. We are a civilised society, after all. Not perfect ... There's always room for malice and deliberate errors ... the metaphorical knife in the back. The barbaric battles are fought overseas ...

The surreptitious malaise of indifference infiltrated our lives. The vacant hours began to appear sporadically. Evenings without our voices. Restless footfalls. The sound of television blunted the intimations of loneliness. The gaps filled with possessions dutifully accepted as important. Bigger house, antique furniture, pedigree pets. A new car to celebrate my promotion. I forged ahead into the dawn of new discoveries. I perceived your presence as a domestic shadow. No more ...

Then the twins arrived. Another beginning. There was joy. A revival. A new direction and purpose ... One morning life slipped out suddenly from the palms of my charmed hands. David died. How simply the doctor explained the reason for our lives being dunked into darkness. Cot death. No-one's fault, he assured us. A regrettable accident. One of those things. Guilt. Self-recrimination. Hysteria and accusations. Corroded, ragged emotions. Exhaustion. I never thought about sharing the hurt. Immersion in my professional life was an antidote. I didn't think about you.

You doubled your efforts with Judy. Maternal vigil. Sleepless nights. I glimpsed the stormy darkness spreading under your eyes. I, too, stopped dreaming about the sun dipping into the sea. There was no desire to be awed by the saffron tinted sky of dawn or to soak up the pleasure of printed words. Once more I gladly entered the vortex of success.

A new life tumbled out of the turmoil. The morning's kiss was like the lightest of touch with sandpaper. Dry and coarse. Monosyllabic politeness became the norm. The myopic satisfaction of professional achievement. Proficiency ... efficiency ... no sentiments involved in retrenchments. It was all kosher ... for the good of the company. Another call from the nineteenth floor. Half-past ten. A brief reminder about the hard times. French champagne to celebrate a job well done. How would I like a new office and a bulkier pay packet? Longer hours, of course.

Of course. The future had to be secured. I was thinking of Judy ... and us. Trusts and equities. Term deposits ... more shares. Brochures from private schools. Anticipated rise in fees ... Forward planning. I was one of those fellows who stamped his intention on what lay ahead. Board meeting, the stock market and long lunches. The amazing drug of power made me surge ahead. The arrogance of invincibility invaded my thinking. Controlled intolerance, mild social prejudices and corporate welfare shaped me. It wasn't all work. There were long hours at the pub. Dark suits, neat haircuts and paunches of prosperity. Mateship and a communal sense of wellbeing.

We talked about serious issues. The achievements of conservatism and the demands of indigenous people. History was not about morality but about charting progress and development. A little too much ethnic diversity out there ... Oh, Chinese and Thai cuisine were fine ... Heck, I wasn't narrow-minded at all. Just a concerned citizen. Why, one of my best mates was a Singaporean, educated at Harvard. I was only in my late thirties and developing.

In the melee of such a busy life, there was no opportunity to pause and ask *Where did love go*?

The late evening's constipated conversation was punctuated with predictable questions and terse replies until it was time for exaggerated yawns. Oh, I spent time with Judy. I was conscious of parental obligations. No-one could question my domestic generosity. Bills paid. No problems about more shopping money. A cleaning lady made sense ... I was a responsible family man.

Relationship? A tangible measurement of life made me oblivious to human needs. I pretended to be excessively tired when you touched me with the uncertain fingers of an acquaintance. The clichéd excuses rolled off readily from my tongue. *I've had a dog of a day ... Early meeting tomorrow ... So tired ...* The hurt of your bewildered silence clogged the darkness. You never allowed the mask to drop in front of others. No symptoms of distress. *We* instead of *I*. Even in my state of preoccupation with myself I admired your strength. Can you possibly believe that my deception was not deliberately intended to hurt?

That's what they all say afterwards ... Whose voice was that?

I was careful not to mention Irene. Despite the regrets, it would be a lie to pretend that I do not remember her with passion. She was more than a mandatory appendage of corporate success.

The late afternoon was cold and misty. There was an open fire ... The warmth surged through me as we talked about floats and property prices. More seriously, there was much to be said about winter's religion. Passions were unleashed, and we were transformed into coaches, players, spectators, analysts ... experts. Tough talk ... slurred speeches and flushed faces. The Shiraz was mellow and expensive ... but it was Friday, and the share prices had gone up during the week.

She appeared from nowhere. Nods, smiles ... hellos. Some resentment at the interruption. Essendon's fortune hadn't been decided as yet. Irene was a divorcee—confident, bold and intelligent, with more than a passing interest in football. Easy to talk to ...

... And after the pain you discover freedom. It becomes your permanent partner. That relationship is to be nurtured above everything else ...

Point taken. Adventures without commitment? Her eyes flashed. *Perhaps. Risks without consequences ...* She worked in advertising, travelled extensively, enjoyed New Age sound and loved the opera. Asian food was definitely on Friday's agenda. She drove a BMW ... The circle widened, and we allowed her to step in.

I love champagne ...

Josh and Nick had to leave. Bruce and Tim lingered over another drink. And then there were two. She knew a Japanese restaurant near where she lived. Dinner was garnished with superficial talk and flirtatious laughter. Irene knew what she couldn't ask. Clever lady. Here and now. *Carpe diem ...* The rest of my life could stay in the darkness outside.

I can make better coffee than they brew here ... Her casual words prevented us from entering a maze. A timesaving statement, alive with implications. The dessert menu was not necessary ...

An astonishing endurance. You suffered without a whimper and began a parallel life—another university course, a part-time job. Two, three years? How cruel it was to batter you with all those late nights without credible explanations. I overheard snatches of the excuses you offered Judy. I was a shadow to my daughter. How much will she be allowed to know? It's in your hands. Will she ever guess how I goaded Fate to punish me?

That night we were soaked in champagne. Careless and fickle. For some reason I couldn't help thinking about you even as I wished Irene the best on her birthday. A frail figure, hunched over a book of verse, reading to an invisible presence, inducing imaginary worlds of perfection. Had I imagined you to be bilious with anger, the celebration might have been without the explosive consequences. But your face ... crumpled ... strained but still patient. The eyes—dim but hopeful. Suddenly the momentous leap from the recklessness of living dreams to the sobering realisation of necessary limitations. A desire to turn and change. A heavy weariness with the world of good living. The champagne tasted flat. The conversation and laughter were irritating. I needed an anchor.

She listened quietly, uncertain whether the outpouring of words resulted from my state of inebriation. I tore down the façade of invincibility. Her silence said it all. Unpredictable. Uncertain. Hypocritical and weak. Yes, yes ... all of those and more.

Sudden endings are the best. That way there is no time to build up a reserve of anger.

I'll take a taxi.

Let me drive you home. Allow me to savour a little self-satisfaction. I have handled this well, I can say to myself as I drive back. The rationality of the modern female. I shall enter loneliness once again with an enviable poise. No, there won't be a scene, I promise. No obligations to make commitments. That was clear from the beginning. Remember?

A relieved silence of release. I wasn't sorry.

The night was wet and treacherous. What did Fate whisper in its ear? As if I believed in such superstition! I remember the landslide of images ... the desperate desire to travel backwards over the years. Then the screech of tires ... breaking glass. Did I reach out with my hands? Did anyone hear what I said before everything snapped?

This is a strange country where I am a reluctant exile. The mist never rises. The voices are always on the other side. A filtered light, but never the sun. I make an effort to speak to the shadows, but their shapes change when they hear me approaching. Sometimes there is a full moon streaked with red and pasted to a winter's sky. Time is severely crippled in the lost land. It hobbles along on regrets and impossible wishes.

Have you returned? Imagine that I am Tithonus pleading with Aurora. *Let me go. Release me.* Haven't they convinced you that I can never go back? Have you exhausted all your courage? There I go again ... expectations that suit me. How long will I hear your voice like an elusive goddess controlling me? Can you reach inside just once to hear what I have to say?

Here I am, roaming through the mist. It is so cold … Why do you sound so angry? Other voices. What has been said to upset you? I can hear a roar. Memory has turned gangrenous. I cannot recall faces … Is that the traveller with the undelivered message? How did he get in? Couldn't he find you? It's important that you know …

No, I won't agree … I know there's little hope. All that I can expect are haggard dawns, weariness and regret. Anger … self-pity. But I won't agree … I won't …

There's that song again …

She was once …

True love? Ah, how could I have possibly known that it had so many dimensions? Frightening … Exhilarating … Massive … Forceful. Like a tidal wave that sweeps away everything in its way. Without reason or light. Suspended somewhere between Eros and Agape. But, in the end, a belief. A tenacious commitment. A lesson … taught by you.

ELIZABETH JOLLEY

Baba: My Song …
Widows and Nephews and all …

Once, when my sister and I were talking together we suddenly realised that out of all the people we had known and knew later, we had known each other longer than anyone else. I know this is applicable to many other people in the same sort of relationship but it is possible that they have never considered the privilege they enjoy. I don't know about my sister, but after that realisation I found I was thinking about her, and feeling grateful that she was my sister; I would remember all kinds of things which other people would not have noticed. Like, for example, the time when we were both under the dining table in our grandmother's house. The table had a big, dark-green plush cloth which hung over the sides of the table so that we were hidden. I had a pair of scissors and I cut off a tuft of my sister's hair. She said to cut more so I did. I took the scissors from one tuft to the next till she had a head of tufty bits of hair. I do not know if this is within her memory or not. Certainly I do not remember that anyone was either pleased or angry about my hairdressing efforts. I do not know if my sister remembers the incident. We were not scolded and sent off to bed. I am sure I would have remembered that …

In spite of hardly ever living near each other as the years have passed and, for some forty years, have had the 'whole world' between us, I suppose I can still regard my sister, even if somewhat taken for granted, as my one true love.

I was told often, when we were growing up, that I must always be kind to my sister. She was my greatest possession, they said. I was very fond and loving towards her. In fact I was told, repeatedly, over the years, that I was the one who had named my sister. It was I who had given her the name, Baba. She grew up with that name even though she had two other names, Madelaine, her saint and Winifred which was chosen by Aunt Daisy. Aunt Daisy apparently chose Sybil first. This name was turned down by our mother who often, whenever the subject was introduced, declared that Sybil was the Queen of the Prostitutes. I have never seen or heard any evidence to support the truth of this rather carelessly uttered dubious fact.

So Baba was how my sister knew herself and it was my name for her. Since I was almost fourteen months old when she was born this name was probably the only sound, a bit like a word, which I could pronounce at that time. She is still known by that name by a few people.

During my life I was often told by elderly people, indicating my height in nearness to the floor by an outstretched hand (palm down) ... *when you were so high* ... that I loved my sister very much. I stood, they said, by her cradle letting no-one come near. And, they said, that very gently I would stroke her soft hair and her soft skin encouraging her to sleep.

My song for my sister was simply her name, Baba, repeated in low growling which they thought must be singing since there were no tears to suggest that I might be weeping.

Later we became partners in childhood. We learned all the ways of childhood together including speech, mealtime behaviour, hot and cold, dry and wet and so on. We had special games which simply grew out of the little walk to the bus stop, or our being together in the same armchair, on the same sofa or in the same bath. Simply from our being together, jumping on the sofa putting the velvet cushions on our heads we leapt on and off the sofa, shrieking, declaring we were widows. In the same way, by declaration we were each other's nephews ... and, by way of taking handbags and hats we were neighbours and aunts.

The slow race was a game which must have infuriated an elderly Mrs Cox who appeared some evenings to put us to bed. To be the last one to finish brushing her teeth was to win the slow race in cleaning teeth. Another game, while Mrs Cox is on the page, was to make a pile of all the soft toys, the teddies, the stuffed animals ... cats and dogs, a giraffe and an elephant (knitted), and to throw them at Mrs Cox as she sat knitting in an armchair, prior to our joint slow bath and our even slower hair brushing.

The slow race with bananas and visiting children was especially rewarding. It was easy to keep a bit of banana hidden in the flapping, apparently empty, peel—and then to bring out the fragment of fruit when the others had finished theirs.

'See if you can get your little sister to go to sleep,' the nurse at the Cottage Hospital said as she took me from my bed to the cot where my sister sat red-faced and crying. The nurse helped me to climb into the cot. There was not much room. 'Lie down, the pair of you,' the nurse said, 'and go to sleep.'

Sharing measles and chicken pox and other illnesses of childhood we were sharing an operation, that of having our tonsils removed.

'Don't close your eyes,' I told my sister, 'let's keep awake. We won't go to sleep.' I can remember thinking that if we did not sleep we should be sent home. I watched my sister as we lay squeezed into the metal cot. Her blue eyes were close to my face, intensely blue. She stopped crying and seemed to look straight into my eyes. Gradually, in spite of my advice, her eyelids closed, slowly opening only to close again. She was asleep. A porter came and, lifting my sister from the cot, carried her, still asleep, away.

And then it was my turn. I was not asleep. The porter pulled a blanket from the cot and wrapped it around me. He called me 'a brave little lady' and told me not to be frightened, and then he carried me away.

Remembering the experience is not pleasant. I understand now that the gas burners we passed must have been under sterilisers. I recall the porter putting me gently on a table. He pulled a thick rubber strap over me and my foot seemed to sink into something soft and cool.

The nurse told me later that I had, by mistake, kicked her in the stomach. 'Not on purpose,' she said then. She said it wasn't on *purpose*. Just an accident.

Once more, as I was waking up, I was put in the cot with my little sister, to see, they said, if I could just 'quieten her down'—before our mother arrived to take us home.

My sister and I often wanted the same book or the same toy at the same time. Our fights (in spite of being taught I must always be kind to my little sister) were frequent. Mostly we grabbed each other's hair and refused to let go. When our mother intervened we joined forces against her.

As we grew older and were separated by the changes in our lives, a kind of reserve or shyness persisted. Perhaps this is normal within families. I have never in later years felt the wish to pull my sister's hair mercilessly, or to grab any of her possessions or even to have an argument with her.

I believe in the love I was told I had for my sister. I am glad I have a sister and it is nice that I was told, years ago (because it is beyond my own remembering), that she was, before I could speak properly, my first concern, *my one true love*.

Just one more note: we are both widows now but restrain ourselves when we are together (which is not often), and we no longer leap about on the furniture.

GRETEL KILLEEN

Luca Luca

I have done two things which will haunt me forever. One of them I will tell you about.

I was forty-seven when I met Luca. I was living in Via Santo Spirito, by the Ponte Santa Trinita, Florence.

I was walking, I think, down the street toward my car, carrying one child and admonishing the other. I was conscious of the green Fiat that drove closely by, because that Fiat belongs to a neighbour of mine, so I looked up to wave and glimpsed the front seat passenger. His chin rested upon his cupped hand and for a moment his eyes burnt me. He was beautiful. So incredibly beautiful … and I now wait for the day when he isn't.

In those times, several years ago, I was so much smarter. I saw him, and I admired him like a fine piece of art. But I did not want to touch. I took my children to school and I'm sure I never would have recalled him again, were it not for the knock on my door.

I didn't know that he was nineteen. 'How ridiculous!' I hear you thinking. But he looked so much older. He seemed so confident. His voice was rich and deep, his posture bold, his shoulders broad, his face strong like a chiselled cliché. In times to come I treated him like my chronological equal, but he was a child in disguise. He said that he was building shelves for my architect neighbour whom he hated. He asked if he could borrow some milk.

His English was perfect. I was dishevelled. I was distracted, self-conscious, curious and dismissive. I gave him the milk, he left, I closed the door, and then I returned to my work. I did not think about him, not *him*, just why I'd given him the last of my milk as I would now have to buy more, venture down the four flights of cold stone stairs and into the cobbled damp street below, to the corner where the fat, rude woman sells milk.

Now, as I scour that terrain of my life, like a metal detector searching for cause and a place to lay blame, I feel guilty. Was I even then, on that very first day, willingly partaking of his game?

Two hours later he returned, with a litre of milk and a fresh hot coffee from the cafe downstairs. He smiled a golden charming smile—wide lips, white teeth—and then he turned and left. His name was Luca and he returned twice more that day. Once to say goodbye in the late afternoon (he did a passing impression of my neighbour the architect which had me laughing like a ticklish child) and once because he said he'd forgotten something. I knew he hadn't. But I searched with him anyway. I don't know why. I wish I hadn't.

I collected my children from school that afternoon. I bathed them, I fed them, I read with them, we laughed. They fought as usual, I tucked them into bed. And then I worked on, like I always do, until late in the night. At 2:00 a.m. I went to sleep, in my bed all alone, like I always do.

Luca was doing something in the hallway early the following morning. I don't think even he knew what. He looked busy, as though not expecting us, but he was humming in that self conscious way of someone pretending to be absorbed in his task ... and unlike yesterday, his sleeves were rolled up high on his muscled arms. His beautiful, beautiful arms.

He met the children, in the hallway, as we hurried off to school. The children, of course, adored him instantly as he used those arms to lift them up high, whirl them around like a funpark ride until all three of them collapsed in a writhing, giggling heap and I was forced to interrupt and say, 'Hurry up, or we'll be late.' He told me I looked beautiful, when in fact, I looked like a harried and frayed single mother of two. I left, offended that he'd been so rude as to mock me.

When he popped in later that morning I was tempered but curt. Life is hard enough, I do my best, I do not need interruptions I do not understand, nor elements I cannot control. 'Yes,' I said, 'what do you want?'

He sensed, as he always would, that yesterday's act would not work today. And so today he apologised for his loud singing next door and enquired if it had distracted me. I said no and closed the door after him because until then I had not heard him sing a note. For the rest of the morning I heard him through the walls and his song became part of my writing.

The day before, as I said, he had visited three times. Today, it was only the once and I wondered why.

I picked the children up from school. I bathed them, I fed them, I read to them, we laughed, they fought as usual, they went to sleep, I worked on. Then I went to sleep, in my bed all alone, just like I always do, but I thought of him.

The following day he was not in the hall and I did not hear him sing. Later I thought I heard occasional hammering but I continued with my work, deleted the influence of his song and forgot him.

Relieved, life was back to normal. I tidied the house, I shopped for groceries, I returned with the children that afternoon and there was an immediate knock on the door. It was Luca casually dressed in jeans and a careless t-shirt, in a look that I now know would have taken him hours to contrive. (I still love you, Beautiful Boy.)

He had brought wine. He'd finished his work next door and had come by to return our neighbour's keys, he'd been paid a bonus and we were to celebrate with him. He begged us to let him cook dinner, then he sang in silly voices and wiggled silly ways as he prepared the pasta sauce, and the children and I sat round the kitchen table, watching his every single move, stifling our adoring laughter.

He fed the children, he read to the children, he tucked them into bed. He disappeared to buy another bottle of wine, so I washed the dishes and turned on the news because I wanted to alert Luca to the fact that this was not a romantic situation. To alert myself, I began scrubbing a saucepan.

He stood on the street below and pulled the rope attached to the bell that rang by our kitchen window. I threw down the keys and, before he entered the apartment, resumed my appearance of pot-scrubbing distraction.

He returned with two bottles of wine, a bottle of cheap champagne and two expensive gold-wrapped chocolates. He poured the champagne and, seeing my hands were occupied, unwrapped my chocolate and prepared to pop it in my mouth. I intercepted him with one suds-spattered pink rubber washing-up glove and shoved the chocolate unglamorously into my own mouth. He dried the dishes as I completed my ridiculous scrubbing.

Luca pretended to dance to the blaring news as he flicked through my CD collection, and finally selected my favourite Marvin Gaye. He wanted me to dance but I was too inhibited. I felt old and gangly as though my exuberant place upon this earth had been replaced precisely by him.

I skolled my champagne. He sipped only slightly from his glass, apparently feeling no need for the liberation of alcohol. Totally breathtakingly in control. He moved through that scene in my life so precisely, so charmingly. I watched in awe of his performance. I was jealous.

(Just as I cannot describe the taste of a mango, so I cannot describe the delight of Luca. I cannot describe his face, so that you might see it, nor his skin that you might touch it, nor his neck that you might taste it, nor his hair that you should smell it, nor his shoulders, nor his back, nor the tremble I felt from my toes to my heart when he laughed, or even said 'hello'. I cannot describe his obscene deliciousness—but I would eat him, I would drink him, I would …)

After three glasses of champagne I watched his brazen, cocky, self-assuredness as he coaxed me onto the wooden floor. I am a good dancer. I'm proud of the way I move. But I was so intimidated by the splendour of Luca that the years of strength and self-esteem I had nurtured were vanquished by his glory.

I said I didn't know how to dance. He said that he would teach me. So to the tunes of Marvin and then Riccardo Vialserre we swung and swayed and laughed and laughed in the room with the window that overlooks the corner where the rude fat lady sells milk. And when the music stopped we kept dancing.

We touched as we moved, I wish we hadn't, but his hands were warm. (Even in the pique of his coldest mood, his hands were always warm.) I tried not to take his physicality seriously. At my age alcohol induced sexual attraction tends to be more embarrassing than arousing. And besides, despite my near drunkenness, I could no way allow myself to be the victim of his older woman conquest. I am damned good at sex but after two children, a divorce, and a small spattering of lovers, who could in the dark be justly mistaken for inanimate objects, I was fearful of competing with Luca's youthful athleticism and sexual confidence.

Typically, he sensed my reservation. 'You look tired,' he said. 'Let's sit for a while.' No-one had cared how tired I was since ... I don't even remember. 'You work so hard, you raise your children, you survive in another country, another language. Here, put your feet up and I'll rub them.' Corny I know, I blame the champagne but he did rub my feet and it was heaven. Pissy, tactile heaven on earth.

To distract myself from the pleasure I asked Luca about his family. To my surprise his was the tale of the poor lost little rich boy, too spoilt he said, never given 'hard love'. And on hearing this, with predictable self righteousness, I sobered up quickly and suddenly hated Luca.

And I hated myself for having been flattered by his attention. I felt polluted by his gaze of three days. Another bored, self-serving male, looking for yet another toy. I never wanted to see him again, nor to have his self-centredness near my life. Those, I believe, who are freely given things in life—love, money, self-worth—do not understand the struggle of those who have had to fight for them. They have no respect for the battles, no awe for the prize.

I was suddenly distant, but he was suddenly more so. He played games so much better than I. I rose as though tired. He rose as though leaving. I walked him to the door, I moved to kiss his cheek goodbye, and he pushed me gently against the wall. He pressed his body hard against me, and his mouth was hard upon mine. Then he said goodnight and left.

Winter was coming to Florence and he went into the cold outside.

I awoke to the ringing telephone. It was Luca of course. It was 3:00 a.m. and he had only just left my apartment. He wanted to thank me for the evening. 'You are lovely,' he said before he hung up, and I started to believe him. Indeed, the following morning I was beautiful.

At 8:00 a.m. the children found our car littered from boot to bonnet with red roses. The roses had adhered with the frost and we left them there as we drove the two blocks to school. I gathered the roses on returning home, placed them in a vase and stood them on the kitchen table. I should have left the roses on the car in the cold, to be more suitably stolen by strangers.

At 9:30 a.m. he arrived with pastries. I said thank you, but I really had to work. He said he understood, and that he wouldn't stay long, he'd make the coffee while I began to write. And he did. He sang quietly in the kitchen, entered my studio with the coffee, and then he fucking left.

I was tired and confused. My life had been interrupted. I spent the morning crying achingly, until who should return at precisely midday with his strong arms and warm hands? I fell into him, steps from my front door and we kissed and folded to the wooden floor. My Luca.

Sometimes I have thought that Luca's plan was to empower himself with my seduction, to conquer me sexually, to win my experienced heart, to flatter himself that he had tamed such an unwilling beast, and then to simply leave. But I do not truly believe him to have been malicious in his courtship of me. I believe he was young and self-obsessed, like a vulture chick feeding upon others to satisfy himself. He wanted a place in the big people's world and I, like the first time a boy gets drunk, was part of his rite of passage.

I have wondered if there was some cultural miscommunication. I have doubted my own instincts, logic, rationale. I have agonised over why I let Luca into my life. I suspect that, for him, I was initially an experience to be had. Perhaps over a period of days, weeks or months but nevertheless he was to remain aloof and unscathed, with a bit more worldly wisdom to his credit. But for all his contrivance, self assuredness and apparent indifference Luca made one simple mistake: he fell in love with me.

It was not the love of compassion, nor sharing, nor respect. It was the love of obsession and I am as much to blame. Obsessional love is the lifeblood of those who are dissatisfied with their lives, desirous of finding a reason for living, hoping to be rescued from life's dullard clutches by a hero or heroine on a white charger.

It has long been said that one cannot love another until one loves and respects oneself. But it is also true that one cannot give true, pure, generous love having never received it, because one quite simply can have no idea of what it is.

Having shared relationships riddled with inequality, jealousy and unbalanced values I have longed, at times in my life to discover and love someone who was just like me. Well, unfortunately, I found him.

• • •

As we lay on our backs, naked on the floor, after that very first time, I curled against his chest, in the shelter of his arms, and he warmly kissed my damp forehead. He yawned, as he was always to do after we had sex, and I felt strangely naughty, safe and cared for as he relaxedly surveyed the walls. His beautiful eyes consumed the room. He liked this painting, he didn't like that wall colour, he queried the rent for an apartment with such a view, and how I managed to find a place in Florence that had its own fireplace. He asked of my relationship with the architect he hated who lived next door. And he clung to my words as I tried to quash the jealousy I suspected by saying that pretentious bow ties like those my neighbour wears make grown men look like clowns. I remember Luca smiled. My answer must have been correct.

Suddenly his eyes ceased to wander and rested instead upon the rich brown wall by the door. It was covered with framed happy photos of good friends, family, funny times, precious pieces of my children's life and mine. 'Who's that?' Luca asked. 'Who's that? Who's that? Where were you then? What's she laughing at? Who's that guy with his arm round you?' I was efficient in my telling. I tried to say the simple truth. I do not believe in lingering over the past. I am what I am as a result of my experience and the past is not consciously my present. 'Did you sleep with him?' continued Luca referring, one by one, to every male on that wall. 'Did you?' he screamed, not hearing the truth, his tortured anguish in my face. 'Did you like fucking him?'

A few, from the past twenty years, yes, I had slept with and I simply could not have cared less. For though I know society foolishly deems sexual relations to be the pinnacle of intimacy, nothing is more intimate, in the truth of my eyes, than shared conversation, shared fears, shared dreams and laughter. That wall was not my well-notched bed post. But when I had finished explaining the details of each and every photo Luca asked me to take eight of them down. And do you know what? I did.

Of course I wonder why. Never before have I negated my existence to substantiate someone else's. But if there was one thing I was too sensitive about, it was Luca's vulnerable youth. At his age I too was threatened by the past of those I cared for and I understood his insecurity, too well I'm sure, for unfortunately I fed it. What I did not understand, and how could I have guessed, was that nothing I ever hid or did would be enough to make Luca feel safe in my life.

For all his apparent puffy self-esteem Luca could never understand his personal magnificence and sheer irreplaceability in my life. Completely unable to accept me as I am now, in the present, Luca was forever dogged and threatened by my past. With his constant interrogations, accusations and snide references he made my past lurid, embarrassing and humiliating when really it was just an average life. I was reviled for a thousand things I had done of little import that he would no doubt, one day, do himself.

In response, I trivialised tales of profound incidents in my life. Old relationships were diluted, loves became likes, affairs became mere experiences. In yearning to construct a precious place for Luca in the patchwork of my life I invalidated my past, and ironically my present. I had seen Luca's wrath so I softened my truth to make him feel safe, and for the rest of our time together these softened truths became lies. Lies which I could not remember, was forced to reconstruct and then ... have the discrepancies flaunted before me.

One's personal perceptions are funny things, so precious yet so easily altered by the repeated subtle threat of mental batterings.

Over the months I began to see my history through Luca's eyes and rather than being proud of who I was and what I had achieved, I grew shameful and appalled at the events of my life. I took the easy route of submission, I doubt it could have been harder. From the start I should have been prouder of who I was, of where I had been, of what I had done. But I wasn't, because in all his splendour I believed Luca to be better than me.

Our sex continued all afternoon. I did no work, which niggled at me but to show respect for Luca, and the uniqueness of the time we shared, I abandoned my day. My time was his and I floated with his life current. I had never been with anyone so beautiful nor wonderful. I hope that I never am again.

Half an hour in advance I told him that I had to collect the children from school and gently rose to dress. He did not appear to hear me, but slowly removed each layer of clothing as I tried to wear it. He did not say a word. He kissed me, he touched me, yes, more sex. I was seven minutes late collecting my children. I had never been late for them ever before. I was angry with him, but only minutely. Mostly I was angry with myself.

The afternoon was chaotic, it was cold and wet, the children were stir-crazy, the dinner burnt, I yelled in frustration. I had written nothing, I had a high profile presentation in one month, I resolved to be more disciplined if and when again I should ever spend time with Luca.

When you're young you can afford to make a relationship your life, because you don't really have much of a life to abandon. But at my age, with my responsibilities and focus, a relationship must fit somehow within the individuals' life structures.

I wrote absolute crap until midnight but by 1:00 a.m. I had begun to work with fulfilling depth and passion. At 1:30 the phone rang. It was Luca. He was outside at the pay phone, had seen my light on and had wondered if I would like some company. Distressed at being disrupted I barked, 'not tonight' but sensing his pain, I weakened, said 'I'm sorry, come on up', and left my writing mid-sentence.

We made love, had sex, blah blah, again and again and again. Then, as the winter sun rose, and I heard my children wake he quietly slipped out the door.

I hated myself as I organised the day. Saturday, all day with the children. I was tired and teary, my children needed me and I needed someone to help. In the morning I took the children to the park. In the afternoon I watched the telephone. He did not ring. As a mother I worried he had not got home safely. As a woman I assumed he was with someone else. In reality he didn't call because he didn't need to. He felt happy and in control of us.

David and Pete, two of my old Australian friends now both painting in Rome, dropped by for dinner that night. A thousand years ago I had shared bumbling sex with Pete, but it was significant only in the fact that men and women often travel through a frustrating sexual relationship to safely reach true friendship on the other side. And so on this night the three of us ate, drank, and laughed, woke the children, then patted them back to sleep.

Luca rang at midnight when he'd finished having his macho boy fun with his mates at Tenax, a bicep flaunting dance club on the periphery of town. He heard the merry voices in the background and asked who was with me. I explained it was David and Pete, old friends from home, and asked Luca if I could call him back tomorrow. Furious he smashed the receiver down and hung up. Over the next hour and a half he rang and hung up on me seven more times. My friends told me he was completely mad, and asked what the hell I was doing letting another 'loop' into my life. This is different, I said. He's worth it.

At 3:00 a.m., after my friends had left, Luca rang in tears and told me to apologise. This need for an apology was an obsession for Luca. Time and time again he was to screamingly demand my apologies—his way of proving that he was right and I had been wrong. His way of extorting power when all he really wanted was a legitimate place in my life. That night I didn't know what I was apologising for but I said sorry anyway. I was sorry that he was hurting, but that was pathetically paltry. 'Say sorry for all that you are!' he should have screamed. 'Say sorry for ever having any sort of life before the day you met me!' It was easier to apologise than justify my existence, but I wish I had just said 'Get fucked'.

At 4:00 a.m. Luca rang the bell. I threw down the keys and awaited his entrance.

His face was full of pain and anguish but he was wild with self-feeding rage. He was objective enough to hate his own jealousy, but without the experience, strength or will to quieten it. He screamed and yelled and I told him to hush because my children were asleep and I didn't want them to wake the same way they had for all those years, before I had left my husband.

I stood apart from Luca and he saw the horror in my eyes. He said he was sorry for being so weak. I held him and comforted him and said, 'It's all right'.

I understood his desperate feeling of inadequacy because I had been there too. I forgave him because I felt revisited by the tortured person I imagined I had been at his age. But I was wrong because in the cold light of now, when I precisely recollect my dysfunctional youth, I realise with most humble clarity I was not a patch on his scattered puzzle-piece performances.

By 5:00 a.m. I was exhausted and of course Luca knew, so he deftly turned the nurturing to me. He made me a tea, something I had taught him, he sat on the couch, he cradled my head in his lap. He told me the story of his cab ride that night. His rendition was brilliant, perceptive and funny. I loved him for making me laugh and feel better, even though it was him that had made me feel sick. He watched me, smiling for a moment and then, stroking my hair, asked again about David and Pete. I said they were friends who just hung about, they were quite nice, not very smart or good looking or successful. I betrayed the depth of my friendships to keep the peace.

I brushed off my behaviour as redeemable. But I was wrong. Only ever start a relationship in the manner in which you wish to continue. I had inadvertently begun to build a house with flawed foundations on unstable ground.

Most of my friends in my life have been men. Soon Luca was to tell me not to see them. 'They want to sleep with you,' he would scream in my face. 'That is the only reason a man has time for a woman.' I began to doubt myself on entirely new fronts. Could I have been so stupid, was I leading my friends on, beguiling them with a possibility, simply because I could not bear the thought of being friendless and alone? I stopped seeing my friends.

Once the rage had subsided I felt safe and very loved. Luca's hands were warm as they stroked my brow and ran softly through my hair. A fine grey rain tapped upon the window sill as a sickly dawn sun slept behind the clouds. We were like normal people for a while, lost in our reverie. We fell asleep and I woke to hear Luca say. 'That vase is very beautiful, who gave it to you?'

It was uncanny how he knew. He rose from the couch, took the vase in his hand and said, 'How dare you put my roses in another man's vase.' I nearly laughed. I was so surprised. I was appalled that I had placed his roses in another man's vase and had not even thought about it. I apologised profusely. I took the vase from Luca and placed it in the bin. 'There,' I said, 'All gone now, that gift meant nothing to me.'

I learnt quickly to surrender to avoid confrontation. I was scared of the boom of his voice, the persistence of his attack and the bottomless vault from which his rage would rise. Strange, because all my friends knew me as a fighter—love, debilitating, suffocating, life-negating love.

I didn't want to know anything about Luca's past loves. Most people are threatened by the romantic experiences of others so I figured the less information I had, the less I had to deal with. Luca, on the other hand, chose to deal with my past by going through it with a fine-toothed comb. He wanted to know about every relationship I'd ever had and importantly he wanted to know why.

It is interesting when you wonder about previous liaisons, why you spent time in your life with this person or that. No-one in my life would be described as nice. Wild, selfish, arrogant, entertaining—Yes. But good, loving, centred people? No, not a one of them. I had something to learn I heard myself say. With that prick? Yes, with that prick.

Luca hated every man I had ever known, few of whom he ever met. Indeed he disliked most of my female friends as well, as though suspecting I did nothing with them but discuss my past and laugh at the foibles of my 'nineteen-year-old boy'. He could not have known how much I simply wanted to be free to love him.

Luca hated the fact that I was, or had ever been, a part of someone else's life—that I would forever appear, even as the smallest stitch, upon someone else's vast life tapestry. But when we had sex, he was king of the world. He conquered all those before him, and rendered obsolete all those I was even yet to meet. We had sex, insatiably. Pure and vital, inimitable. It was the only way we ever honestly communicated, the uncorrupted essence of Luca with the absolute essence of me. That is why I guess we fell in love, because with no-one else had either of us ever been so free to be our essential selves.

We met every day, often several times. We made love at least once every single time we saw each other. In the house, in the car, in the fields, in the antiquated rattly apartment lift, in the foyer, in a dark alcove walking home from the cinema, rarely if ever in my bed. Obsessed.

Sometimes he would ask to sleep with me in my bed but I would always say no to protect my children. I didn't want the turmoil of my existence with Luca to enter my children's lives. Luca felt that this displaced him and I should imagine it did. It made our night times secretive and always hurried, even if the time spent together lapsed over hours. This created added pressure ... it exhausted me ... but my children were to remain protected from the intensity of his love. One month after we met Luca asked my children if they'd ever seen Mummy in bed with a man.

Did I think the relationship would last? I didn't know if it was a relationship. One day it was to be forever, the next day Luca was slamming doors, spitting vitriol and storming from the apartment. One day he would speak of our undying love, the next I was a liar who respected no-one, thought only of herself and could never be trusted. Fucking, slut, bitch he'd say as his rage exploded. I didn't mean that, he'd say, as he calmed.

So why, if it was so debilitating, did I ride the turbulent waves of our time together? Because when I saw him my heart quavered. And when the abuse stopped, when the storm passed, the calm in comparison was all the richer. There were happy times too, careering bike chases round Piazza della Signoria, a surprise celebration of my birthday at least every three months. Once in a while my children would stay some nights with my friend Anna, and Luca and I would sleep in the woods of Liguria, fish in Trani, ski at Madonna Di Campiglio, sing loud karaoke duets in Venice. But were I to be invited somewhere socially with Luca he would plague workmates or friends with questions regarding their relationship with me. Were I to go out socially without him he would start a fight to ensure I was late and that my night was ruined.

I just loved him, perhaps you understand.

I forgave him his insecurity because he was young, and because I was older and more experienced. I took responsibility for the relationship and determined to make him feel secure. In doing so I only made things worse. I gave him a set of keys to the apartment.

I don't know why I bowed to him during that time. Sometimes I think it's because I knew that for all his bravado I was really the stronger one. I felt that I could cope with the disruptions better than he. I accommodated him because I could. I blame the mother in me. I think also that in previous relationships I had been guilty of becoming bored, of 'eating them up and spitting them out' and I had wanted to change that pattern in my behaviour. I perhaps was also in love with a notion ... with someone who simply did not exist. Many of us are guilty of that one.

For two years I tried to prove my love both to Luca and myself and achieved nothing more than a further entanglement within my web of lies. I lost confidence. I needed nurturing. Miraculously the children continued to thrive. I stopped writing. We lived off my savings. But when life was good it was very, very good ... living the most passionate romance.

Up and down, up and down for two agonising years. And whenever I got too far down, and knew in every aching cell of my body that I could no longer live like this, Luca would reach out his Statue of David hands, lift me back up to stand by his side, tell me I was beautiful, wonderful, talented—only to beat me down again when I appeared to get too strong and Luca would begin to fear that I might no longer need him.

Of course I was not perfect.

Luca hurt, cried and loved as I did—for much of the time our love was agonising to him. We were trapped. Mad rats in a cage.

I believe that Luca's love for me was so destabilising to him that the only way he could deal with it was to try and make it go away, to actually rid me from his life by proving that I was not worthy of his love. Hence the relentless persecution, designed somewhere subconsciously in his magnificent mind to weaken me until I broke and then became the very liar and cheat that he had always accused me of being. But that is his story and he can tell it.

I always believed that things would change and get better because I thought it wasn't possible to go through all we had together and to have nothing to show in the end. I was wrong.

One Saturday morning while I was out taking the children to soccer, Luca searched through the back of my wardrobe. (He would often pry in my belongings.) He found a pretty box containing a lace bra. It was twelve years old, a gift from an old boyfriend, and had never, ever been worn. But that night after dinner the questions began, the accusations, the relentless battering, over such a simple thing. I asked Luca to be quiet for the sake of the children. He told me I sounded like his mother and threw me into the wall. With bleeding nose, broken arm and two broken ribs I ignored his sobbing apologies, took the children and, I don't know how, drove myself to the local hospital.

He rang the following morning to say we needed time to learn how to be together. I did not imagine we would ever speak again.

After the accident our neighbour started dropping by to help. He was the architect Luca so hated and his name was Riccardo. He was not my Luca but he was good to us. Life was not exciting with him, but it was fine, he was very loving, though I did not love him.

We didn't touch one another for eleven months until one night, after too much wine, we had very bad sex on the couch. We dressed, shared a coffee, sat fumblingly discussing the cold weather outside and uncannily after all his absence and silence, Luca chose to ring.

'Who's there?' he said. 'No-one,' I replied. And I knew Luca was ringing from the pay phone on the corner where the fat rude woman sells milk.

I did not think. He had the keys. I heard them slide into the lock on my door. Riccardo sat beside me, our two wines on the table before us, I rose to meet Luca, not thinking of the consequences, knowing it was my Luca coming home and just longing to see him once more. He entered and surveyed the room, his lip curled, his body trembled, he looked at me with filthy disgust and from the fire selected a glowing red log, picked it up with his bare, warm Statue of David hands, shoved it into Riccardo's eyes and then beat Riccardo until he only twitched. And Luca fell sobbing to the ground, saying, 'I'm sorry, I'm sorry, I'm sorry.' And I replied, 'I love you.'

I try to make myself hate Luca. I imagine I see him in the streets every day, though I know he won't be around for at least eleven more years. My friends tell me time will make me forget. But it won't. The day he rings me, I will speak to him. Should he ask me to visit, I will. I long to have him touch me one more time. I hope he dies where he is.

José Borghino

Monsieur Poltarac Eats Cheese

Mirabelle Chandos was searching through her cookbooks for the gratinée recipe when she remembered Monsieur Poltarac's abhorrence of cheese.

She tried to think of a way around the impasse. She could cook him a separate dinner, or she might do without the cheese just this once, or perhaps she should just abandon the gratinée altogether. But this need of hers to make the gratinée was no childish whim. All week a vague desire had haunted her like a second body, wheedling from inside her, stammering towards a name. Then this morning—just before she woke up—she had smelled the word, tasted it slipping down her throat and filling her like a child in a womb. She had sat up in bed and spoken the word first to herself and then out loud, 'Gratinée'.

And yet, despite this sign, here she was actually contemplating the possibility of not making gratinée at all tonight! And for what? For the sake of a fastidious prig whose dietary obsessions had come to dominate life at the Chandos Boarding House for Young Christian Gentlemen. Sometimes it seemed as if Monsieur Félix Poltarac's innards had been spread out across the dining room table and mapped nightly since he had first arrived only a month ago. At every meal, if he did not complain of being allergic to one or another of the ingredients of Mirabelle's soup, then it would be his latest specialist diet which prevented him from even sampling the meat dish, and if it was not that then it would be some traumatic memory from his childhood or from his recent travels which impelled him to push the dessert away with one hand while raising his other as if about to bless the fruitbowl. 'Madame Chandos,' he would intone, 'I regret to say that I cannot partake of the mouthwatering delights of your soup/roast/trifle tonight. You see …' And a story would unwind itself like a tapeworm from his gut and settle like a curse over the entire meal.

No! Mirabelle Chandos would not let him do it again tonight. This stripling. This milk-fed upstart, more delicate than an infant and more cantankerous than a grandmother. What did he know about food? About life? True, his stories were often rousing and touching in a melodramatic way. He claimed to have travelled the world and been involved in adventures that belied his years and his delicacy. But for all Mirabelle Chandos knew, Félix Poltarac might be a devious liar as well as a cloying, lily-livered annoyance.

She shuddered at the thought of him. The arrogance of the man—refusing at least one course of every meal she had ever placed before him. Other men travelled for days to sample her cooking. The whole town deferred to her on matters gustatory and the chefs at all three of the town's best-appointed restaurants regularly asked her for advice and even a recipe or two, now and then, when they had plumbed the depths of their own experience and needed fresh inspiration. She was famous throughout the province. It was even said that her name was whispered with reverence in the best kitchens of Paris.

Indeed, not so long ago, just after the end of the war, when she had been a widow only twelve months, there had been weekly offers from chefs and restaurateurs. She could have sold the Chandos Boarding House to join a dozen establishments as a full partner. And some of these offers had included the hint of other types of partnerships, other kinds of joinings—never in a disgusting or offensive way, of course, but with oblique references, nevertheless, to the 'natural needs' of a young woman cruelly separated by war from the love and attention of her husband so soon after their wedding. And, without fail, the suitors would commend the bravery or the beauty or the bonhomie of Staff Sergeant Pierre-Lucien Chandos, Croix de Guerre, tragically cut down by a German bullet at the age of twenty-six at Verdun, 1917.

Mirabelle smiled at the picture of Pierre she kept next to her beloved recipe books. It had been taken at their wedding. He looked so handsome that day she thought her heart would shred into confetti. She remembered their nights of love together. She remembered every meal she cooked him. And she remembered the night he received his call to the Front. They were entwined together in bed but they did not make love that night. Pierre had held her a long time as she lay crying. He suddenly threw the bedclothes to the floor and with a look that combined childlike joy and an unspeakable sadness, he had softly said, 'Let me savour you, let me drink you in, one last time.'

And so they had watched each other breathe for hours. And she had stopped crying.

The memory of that night gave her courage. She would confront Monsieur Poltarac with a vengeful gratinée of monstrous proportions and he would have to eat it or leave her house immediately. She would do it tonight.

That night the dining room was filled with a strange expectancy. The other boarders had sensed vibrations in the air and, without the slightest sign from Mirabelle, one by one they all came down to dinner wearing their finest clothes. Even Monsieur Robert Degasse, the local organiser for the railway union who usually made it a point of honour to dine in his work clothes, had chosen to wear his Sunday church-going best. All of Mirabelle's regulars, her 'boys' as she called them, were there. Monsieur Eugène Durix, the Departmental school inspector, had arrived that morning and was full of high spirits, chattering to the other guests about some scandalous affaire de coeur he had discovered at a school in the previous town he had visited. Monsieur Jean-Claude Platini, the booksellers' representative who visited every month and brought Mirabelle the latest romances so she could read them before anyone else in town, laughed with his usual gusto. 'There's a book in you, Monsieur Durix,' he said. 'By God, there's a bestseller!' Not to be outdone, Monsieur Platini then revealed the latest news from literary circles in the capital, stories of inflamed passions and secret duels at dawn, of youthful promise trampled and of love triumphant.

Mirabelle only half-listened to these stories—she had not been so absorbed in the preparation of a meal for years. There was a smooth urgency in her movements as she brought in side dishes and plates from the kitchen. Candles flickered drowsily at both ends of the table. Squat bowls filled with freshly-picked camellias guarded the base of each candelabra. Even the cutlery and wineglasses, by no means ever dull or unpolished, seemed animated by an extra sparkle.

Félix Poltarac sat at his usual place, smiling nervously as always. Mirabelle watched him as she brought in the decanted wine and the crystal jug of lime water and placed them in the centre of the table. His slim hands opened and closed abstractedly on either side of his dinner setting. She had admired his hands when he had first arrived. Smooth and hairless, with long, almost luminous fingers and fine, transparent nails. Bordering on the feminine. They reminded her of willow leaves. So unlike Pierre's, and yet, to her surprise, she had realised that she liked them.

Monsieur Poltarac wore his usual dining clothes: a dark blue suit that accentuated his blue eyes and his black, always meticulously combed hair; a white, perfectly laundered shirt; and a blood-red silk cravat. He always dressed in a serious, conservative fashion that only served to underline his youth. How old was he? Her age, perhaps? Sometimes he looked younger but he always acted older.

Félix Poltarac was watching her that night. She could feel his eyes upon her as she distributed napkins around the table. She caught herself smiling. She remembered the times before their marriage when Pierre would pay her parents unexpected visits and she would cook a spontaneous feast, and how he would tease her with little comments about the consistency of the sauce or the texture of the vegetables. And how flustered she became as her father bellowed, 'At last, a truly brave man who criticises the celebrated Cuisinière of the Valley even as he woos her!' And her brothers and sisters all laughed and gave each other sly looks as she felt her face redden with rage.

Pierre had confessed on their wedding night that his criticisms of her cooking had been baseless and that he had made them only to clear a way to her heart. 'To force you to think of a man rather than your pots and pans,' he had said.

Well, she thought to herself, Monsieur Poltarac would never forget her pots and pans, not after tonight, that much was certain.

The boarders sat around the table with high hopes of a feast to remember. The simplest of meals at the Chandos Boarding House were delicious, but tonight the food would undoubtedly be extraordinary. Madame Chandos had been noticeably exhilarated, filled with some new found spirit. Was it a secret anniversary, the old-time boarders asked themselves, an intimacy she would share with them through that medium in which she had no rival—food?

When the table was set, Madame Chandos stood at the head of the table to announce, as she always did, the night's menu. Tonight she began at the end, with the dessert *poires à la Bourguignonne,* and then the main course *côtelettes d'agneau chasseur.* She had purposefully chosen a dessert and main course that Monsieur Poltarac had previously deigned to consume. The other boarders registered their delight with polite applause, or by raising their glasses in salute, or with a good-humoured smacking of lips.

'Before I announce the soup of the day,' she said, 'I wish to institute a new and binding house rule. All of you gathered here tonight know the love with which I prepare even the rudest meal and the satisfaction I gain from the sight of a table of guests vigorously appreciating the results of my labours. It has been increasingly disappointing for me to observe that this appreciation is not unanimous. From tonight, all dinner guests will be required to consume all three courses of every meal I prepare. If they do not, then they are free to leave.'

With that Mirabelle Chandos flourished the lid of the soup tureen and proclaimed, 'The soup for tonight is *soupe à l'oignon gratinée.* Your bowls, please gentlemen.'

Mirabelle Chandos felt slightly ridiculous, the tureen lid in one hand and a ladle in the other, the sharp smell of melted gruyère wafting from the tureen in thick, steamy clouds.

Félix Poltarac stared ahead, immobile and impassive. None of the other boarders dared move, they looked first at him and then at each other. Slowly, decisively, Monsieur Poltarac took his soup bowl in both hands and lifted it from the table. He offered it to Mirabelle Chandos.

'To the brim, Madame,' he said.

Mirabelle Chandos filled his bowl and handed it back, trembling. Félix Poltarac unfolded his napkin and spread it across his lap. With precise and unadorned gestures he raised his spoon and began to eat the soup. He did not look up and he did not hesitate. He finished the entire bowl, placed the spoon in it, re-folded his napkin on the table and sat back.

He pushed his chair back and stood up. 'Thank you, Madame Chandos,' he said without looking at her. 'The gratinée was delicious. I will be packed and gone by the morning.'

He turned to the rest of the table and bowed slightly. 'Goodnight, gentlemen.' With that he walked out of the dining room and ascended the staircase.

Mirabelle Chandos could not sleep. She lay in her bed, sick at heart and filled with remorse. What had she done? What could she have been thinking of? An evening that was to have been her triumph had turned instead into a humiliating disaster. The look on Félix Poltarac's face as he ate her soup came back to her again and again—his look of resignation as he left the room.

His hands had not trembled once, his voice had not wavered. His deep blue eyes were fixed and empty as if he were about to climb out of a trench. Mirabelle thought of Pierre under his tombstone at the cemetery. She remembered his face the night they spent watching each other on this bed, his hands slowly caressing her skin.

And she began to weep. Her body emptied itself of all the tears she had not cried the day Pierre's body had arrived on the train from Paris, all the tears she had not shed when they had lowered him into the muddy earth, all the tears that had remained frozen in her heart for three years since. And a new instinct began to form inside her, a clean new understanding. And with it, a sudden resolve.

She got up. Put on her nightgown. She walked along the corridor and up the staircase to Félix Poltarac's room. She opened the door without knocking, closed it behind her and moved to the side of the bed, letting her nightgown fall to the floor.

But the bed was empty. He was gone.

On the night-table was a note and a photograph.

My dearest Mirabelle,
I have wanted to call you that for so long. Let me say it to you,
now, for the first and last time.

Monsieur Poltarac Eats Cheese

Although I had never met you until a month ago, I have known you for much longer. Your beloved Pierre was my sergeant at Verdun, and I his lieutenant. We fought together for only a short time, but in that time he talked to me often of you. The night before he died, he gave me a photograph he carried with him and he asked me, if I should survive the morning attack and he did not, to visit you to return this photograph and to tell you how he loved you and how he had always carried you within him.

I was wounded in the attack and upon release from hospital I wandered the world trying to exorcise the ghosts that haunted me from that time. I carried your picture with me for Pierre's sake, but in time I knew I had to return it to you.

When I arrived here after my wanderings, I expected to stay but a few days and then be on my way. But I fell in love at the first sight of you. Perhaps it was the stories Pierre had told me of your courtship or perhaps it was your obvious sadness and grief, years after Pierre's death, that moved me as much as your beauty and grace. But you could not see my love, you were so filled with Pierre. So I contrived to court you the way Pierre had done. I thought that if I refused the hospitality of your food, that you would once again notice a man. I realise now the madness of such dreams and I ask your forgiveness for the embarrassment and pain I have caused you.

I return to you the picture that Pierre-Lucien Chandos entrusted to me. But know, Mirabelle Chandos, that I love you and that I will always carry you inside me.

Félix Poltarac

Robert Drewe

The Boy the Colour of Sand

Lots more things go through my head these days. As you'd expect. But the one I keep thinking of is my boy saying 'starfish'. That's what he said to me the last time.

When I see that day it's stretching out in three sharp colours—yellow and blue, and then the river a milky green like an aquarium, full of things you can't quite see. A warm Saturday afternoon in late January. The twenty-sixth, actually, Australia Day. The reason I know the date is because the papers brought it up later.

We're at Crawley, sitting on that strip of sand between the grass and the river, near the tea-rooms. There's quite a big crowd, *mostly families*, with old people and little kids and a few New Australian boys showing off with a soccer ball. There's a few radios playing. A lot of people prefer the river to the ocean. People with little kids, New Australians and other people scared of the surf.

We're half in the shade of some sort of flowering gum. I've sat my boy in the shade so he won't get burnt. But there are these tree roots poking up, and ants, and the shade keeps moving, and he keeps squirming out into the sun again, so I've got to put zinc cream on him. The other kids have quickly shot through. They're way down the beach, doing bombs off the jetty.

He's the usual mess. The paddlepop I've bought him is melting fast. It's dripping all over him, mixed up with sand and zinc cream. I'm trying to wipe him with a towel but of course he's twisting away.

Suddenly he stops wriggling, looks straight at me and says 'starfish'. Clear as a bell.

What? I can't believe this is a proper word he's said. 'Yes!' I say. 'Right! Starfish!' Then I take a breath and ask him quietly, 'Where's the starfish?'

Crawley's nine or ten miles up-river. Not many starfish that far from the sea. I've never seen one anyway. None there this day either, and nothing on the shore that you'd mistake for one. But him saying the word gets *my* hopes *up* for a moment, even after all this time. It makes me think things might be changing in his brain.

For a few seconds there on the beach things are pretty strange. I forget his mucky face. He seems *on the ball*. There's another thing. While he's saying 'starfish', he's staring deep into my eyes. His look is sort of wise, like he's looking right into my head.

This isn't just looking back and imagining things after they've happened. The picture's so clear. It's still as sharp to me as five minutes ago. I bet my nerves showed. In a way I was more jumpy then than I am now.

'Good boy!' I said. My voice sounded enthusiastic and fake, like a radio announcer's. 'Thinking about starfish? That's the boy!' I was desperate to keep the moment *going. To* draw it out. *So* I quickly scratched a star in the sand.

'Look,' I said. 'A starfish.' But my starfish didn't register. The wise look was fading off his face. The blind was coming down again. That's the only way I can describe it. Like shutters, that's how it seemed to me. The focus had gone out of him. The way he looked at me now was just his *old* lights-on-but-nobody-home look. Then he started making the old bossy noises that meant he wanted something else right away, and bloody hurry up about it.

Everything drained out of me. I could've cried. Whatever it was he wanted, I couldn't be bothered trying to catch on. It could've been anything. Bring me those seagulls! Let me drive that speedboat!

He stacked on a real tantrum, like a two-year-old in a supermarket. I pretended to ignore him but you can't, of course. Ice-cream in his eyebrows and ears and trickling all down his chest. People were turning around at the racket and giving me snaky looks. I grabbed him up, a bit rough, and carried him into the river and kept walking.

The river was just stirring up with the sea breeze and afternoon tide. Underfoot it was all oozy silt and algae, and colder than it looked. My legs were shaky. But, Jesus, I was determined.

For a while he kept kicking up a fuss, then when the water got deeper he clung on tight, moaning and *hanging on for dear life*. It took a while but I kept wading out until it was up to my chest and deep enough to submerge us both, and I did.

When we came up he was coughing and sobbing, but then he went quiet and just held on tight all the way back. I felt like a bastard but I was still so bitterly disappointed I was numb. As I waded into shore I felt like I'd been swindled by the world's most twisted conman. A real sadistic bastard, that God.

Back on the beach he stayed well behaved, squatting at the water's edge, playing his sandy little games. I took some deep breaths and made an effort to get over the way I was feeling. Get a grip, I thought. He is who he is. He's my boy. Be thankful for small mercies—at least the bloody ice-cream's washed off him.

His games were such solemn bits of nonsense. You couldn't help your heart going out to him. I *sat* there all afternoon watching him carefully placing mussel shells in a hole and jabbing jellyfish with a stick. I studied him *real* hard. While he was busy and frowning away to himself I really tried to understand what made him tick.

Small for nine. Thinner than the younger kids, more pointy looking and paler. Not *abnormal* abnormal—just *the* far side of normal. You noticed his knees and elbows more, and the way his legs bent out to the sides. The other kids were as brown as berries but as I watched him it struck me he was the same colour as the sand.

Everything about him—his pale hair, his skin, even his faded khaki shorts, blended right into the sand. He was like one of those little sand crabs. Now you see them, now you don't. If you leaned back a bit and half-closed your eyes, the beach absorbed him. Soaked him right up. He hardly had an outline. He was nearly invisible. If it wasn't for his jerky little movements and his noises *you wouldn't know* he was there.

• • •

A man who had worked for my father at Dunlop Rubber, delivering tyres and car batteries and fan belts to wholesalers, turned out to be a murderer.

A truck driver during the week, and a prowler and cat burglar on Friday and Saturday nights, he'd killed eight people, most of them sleeping, and all of them strangers to him, in the late fifties and early sixties.

Because of his varied modi operandi: shooting, strangling, stabbing, hatchet blows, and murder by motor vehicle (stalking, then deliberately running down a young girl with a car), plus his wide range of victims, both males and females, from the ages of seventeen to fifty-four, the police had been convinced they were looking for several different killers.

We lived in a small, remote and conservative city where people knew each other's business; a normally placid place whose cohesive social network was jolted, terrified and bemused by the successive murders. (An example of the extreme police desperation: all the males over the age of fourteen living west of the city were fingerprinted. I was one of them.)

But once the murders had been sheeted home to one insignificant-looking truck driver, now safely captured, convicted and awaiting execution, an interesting phenomenon swept the city, and especially the middle-class coastal suburbs which had been his primary target.

As the murderer waited for the morning of his hanging, people tried to outdo each other in their claims, if not of kinship (no-one wanted to claim that), then at least of a firm and everyday connection to him.

Suddenly there was a macabre sort of kudos in having once worked alongside him (or even being related to someone who had) at one of his many brief jobs: at Krasnostein's Scrap Metal, for instance, or the city fruit and vegetable markets or, indeed, at Dunlop Rubber. So it wasn't too surprising that, like many others who had grown up with the string of murders in their midst, I easily found several points of connection to the murderer.

I thought my links were closer than most. They were hard to beat. To begin with, he'd killed a friend of mine. And I'd known the murderer. There were those conversations between us in my teens, when his deliveries to and from our house coincided with my mooching around the yard or back verandah.

Perhaps because it was the most nonsensical of our cryptic chats, I remembered the first one most clearly. I was fifteen. It was the summer school holidays. I'd been mending a puncture in the tube of a bike tyre—the puncture had delayed my heading for the beach—and while I waited for the patch to set I was impatiently pumping the bicycle pump against my arm and making that squeaky sound.

Suddenly this short, dark man strolled around the corner of the house carrying a box of flooring tiles. He was humming that Frankie Laine song, 'Sixteen Tons'. 'Don't do that,' he said as he came up to me. 'You'll give yourself warts.'

He had a hare-lip, and a cleft-palate nasal voice. He was about thirty. His eyebrows met in the middle.

'Really,' I said eventually.

'My word, yes,' he said. He was smiling and frowning at the same time.

'I don't think so,' I said, although I stopped what I was doing.

In the connection stakes, however, there was that vastly more serious link. My friend was nineteen and studying agriculture at the university when he was killed.

On that particular hot summer Saturday night in his student boarding house he and another boy had tossed a coin for the bed on the open back verandah. My friend won the toss. While he was asleep, the murderer crept up to his bed and shot him in the head.

Another connection was that long before we knew he was the murderer, we suspected he'd prowled our house at night when my father was away on his annual sales trip to the north-west.

My father used to travel by cargo ship up the coast, stopping off at all ports to take wholesale orders for Dunlop tyres and Dunlopillo mattresses and Volley sandshoes and Maxply and Slazenger tennis racquets and Dunlop-65 golf balls and scores of other products. His sales trips took eight weeks. Everyone at the company knew when he was away.

My mother woke at the noise of her bedroom window being opened at two a.m. She had the presence of mind to shout at the prowler to go away. 'I'm calling the police.' (She told me this later, and that she thought she recognised him by his hare-lip. At the time she'd not wanted to wake me and involve me in 'trouble'. Or been positive enough to name him to the cops.)

There were other thrillingly grisly, if tenuous, links. For instance, the hatchet he'd used to kill one young woman, a chocolate heiress, had come from the garage of another friend of mine. He'd stolen it while prowling my friend's house earlier that night. My friend, helping in the garden, had used the hatchet that afternoon to trim the lawn edges. (His fingerprints were still on it, which took some explaining to the police. The murderer, it would turn out, always wore women's kid gloves.)

And then the final murder in the series, the shooting of an eighteen-year-old girl, a science student at the university, killed on the sofa where she'd fallen asleep over her textbooks while babysitting, had taken place in the street behind our house.

There was a final connection. Having become a newspaper reporter in the intervening years, I later covered his murder trial. I looked up at him sitting in the dock; he looked down at me sitting at the Press table.

Anyway, when they'd finally caught him, he confessed at once to all the murders. At his trial, his lawyer tried to convince the jury he'd been insane each time. He questioned him on his cruel childhood: the beatings from his father, the teasing about his hare-lip. From Grade One he'd been suspended from every

> school he attended. Several times he'd been hospitalised for severe head injuries. Twice psychiatrists had admitted him to psychiatric hospitals for observation.
>
> 'When I shot the boy on the verandah, I thought I was God,' he told the court. The jury didn't buy it. After only an hour's deliberation they found him sane, and guilty.
>
> I wasn't sure whether I bought it or not. But I couldn't get him and the murders out of my mind. My adolescence was steeped in them, and my mind and imagination remained so.

So when I remember that day, it's the afternoon that's on my mind more than the night. The afternoon, and the evening between.

The evening seems to move in slow motion. I take the kids home from the beach on the bus. Hand them over to the wife. I shower, get dressed. See you later. The car's at the panel beaters so I catch the bus into town. (Not that I'd take my car anyway on a Saturday night!)

It's still light as I get off the bus and walk up the Terrace. The day's in that sunset neutral time. The sea breeze has dropped, the easterly hasn't quite begun to blow. It's like the evening's drawing breath, as if it could go either way. Holding fire.

The sun's hanging low over the river. It's over the coast, over Cottesloe, over Peppermint Grove. A reddish-golden glow over those big shady houses among the peppermint trees.

Funny, you never notice the peppermints around our way. Our council trees are mostly Queensland Box. We've got a few peppermints here and there. Their leaves smell the same when you rub them in your fingers, but the council prunes our trees pretty savagely. Back to the bloody trunk. Our streets aren't shady and secretive. There's nowhere to hide, that's for sure.

In town I go bowling as usual. An hour at Fairlanes to keep my hand in. Then across to the Savoy to see *And God Created Woman*. Brigitte Bardot in one bath towel after another, and in bed with sheets pulled up tight to her armpits. Of course you can't see anything. I walk out before the end. I've got better things to do.

I have a shandy at the pub.

I call in to see Mum and say hello.

I steal a car and drive around for a bit.

• • •

I park in a quiet street and walk around the side of a house.

A man and woman are watching TV in the front room. I go in through the back door. On a bedroom dresser there's a few notes and coins which I take. In a cupboard there's a .22 rifle, plus ammunition. I knock them off too.

I drive to the ocean to see what's doing. Pretty dark, not much of a moon. You can barely see the Rottnest lighthouse. Down by the sea at Cottesloe there's a man and a woman in a parked car. I come closer to see what they're doing. The man sees me having a look. He swears at me and throws a beer bottle.

I aim the .22 and shoot at them. There's screams and the car accelerates off, all over the road. The whole evening speeds up into night time. Now I'm feeling serious. I drive around. I go into places with the gun.

The murderer was the father of seven children. His eldest child, a nine-year-old boy, was mentally retarded. While the father was in prison awaiting execution, the boy went on a picnic excursion to the river, wandered away from the supervising adults, and drowned.

The prison authorities wouldn't allow the prisoner to attend his son's funeral. Surprisingly, he seemed to take the decision calmly. Shortly after the boy's death he went just as calmly to the gallows.

In the days just before he died, according to those who last saw him: the prison superintendent, the Methodist chaplain, his mother and his wife, he apologised for his crimes. They remarked on how philosophical and uncharacteristically talkative, even optimistic, he seemed.

MIKE COWARD

India

Perhaps it was naivety. Or foolishness. Or the cursed blindness which prevents introspection.

Whatever, at least now, two-thirds through this incarnation should the Force be benevolent, I can see my true love for India must have long lain dormant. For such is its power, surely it cannot have materialised when memories of uncomplicated and unthreatening days have grown distant.

Against my better judgement there is a gnawing need to know when India entered my consciousness.

'Why do you need to know?' asks an Indian acquaintance whose easy acceptance of all things is as enviable as it is disarming.

'Probably because I am not Indian,' I reply with more confusion than conviction.

'Are you not?'

I'm not Indian. At least, I don't think so. My adoptive parents have never suggested so. But then again, from what you hear, the authorities kept more than the unsuspecting adoptee close to their chest in the 1940s. After all, I am swarthy, and I have been taken for an Indian. And an Italian. And an Israeli. And, occasionally, an Australian.

And while I'm aware Colonel His Highness Shri Sir Ranjitsinhji Vibhaji, Maharajah Jan Sahib of Nawanagar, GBE, KCSI (Ranji) is a semi-divine, although he played cricket for England and not India, I'm two years too old to have been a love child of any member of the first Indian Test team to Australia.

Regrettably, this was patently obvious whenever I went into bat. Nevertheless, I confess to having dreamed of being the accidental Test batsman with the flourish of an Amaranth, Hazare or Mankad.

My parents, now very senior citizens, recently transferred from an independent unit to semi-independent accommodation at a retirement village in Adelaide. The finality of the move struck at the heart and cautioned me to decelerate and reflect.

Mother's precious bits and pieces which once competed for space with the good china and the canteen of cutlery in a heavy, carved, felt-lined blackwood sideboard turned up in a worn and unlidded shoe box jammed among linen in a built-in wardrobe.

The urge to look through the contents was irresistible and I propped awkwardly on the coarse carpet and with childlike anticipation embarked on a voyage of rediscovery. It was evident soon enough that the box contained nothing that had not previously been discussed or proudly paraded at family gatherings. Yet in a sense, there was a freshness to the contents, as the box had been out of mind as well as out of sight for too long.

There were photographs, certificates, ribbons, pins, letters, some bearing half-penny stamps, others with wax seals, newspaper cuttings and, as it happened, an essay I had handed in as a nine- or ten-year-old in Grade V at Brighton Primary School.

It had been written with a rough if reasonably confident hand with a pen that had been dipped in ink. And judging by the tiny lacerations on the page the nib had needed replacing. A cursory glance at the writing with its exaggerated loops for Ls, Gs and Fs, was sufficient for one word to leap from the page. India.

I read with some incredulity my childish ramblings of wanting to go to India to make a difference among those suffering great privation. China was mentioned but clearly India was the reason for the essay.

It is at times like this I wish I had strong recall of boyhood. But I remember little of my formative years and have no idea why India seems to have been writ so large in my young life. Perhaps it had something to do with the Congregational Church of the day and its hot gospelling about intrepid overseas missionaries.

Or is there a spiritual connection with India which I can neither understand nor explain?

It was twenty-six years after penning that childhood essay before I reached India for the first time.

Travel literature is replete with first impressions of India. This is a seminal moment in the life and times of any traveller and reactions and responses invariably reflect the conflicting characteristics and vagaries of this extraordinary and ancient land.

In all honesty I cannot say I felt I had reached my spiritual home. Probably because I do not know my personal history I have no true understanding of the connection with place. I'm unearthed, as it were. Yet while I had entered a world of such different sights, sounds, smells, values, and virtues I did not feel out of place. And nothing has changed in the sixteen years which have followed and I respond regularly and happily to India's constant beckoning.

As earnestly as I try, I can comprehend little of her history and politics and ritualised religious and social customs yet, somehow, I seem to have an innate understanding of the rhythms and moods of the country.

It may seem presumptuous but this is how I feel. And deeply. Perhaps Ganesh, the wondrous elephant-headed Hindu god invoked at the start of all literature and renowned for removing obstacles, has cleared a path for me. As it is, I unselfconsciously carry his carved image in my travel bag and other likenesses are to be found around the home. I may not perform any elaborate puja in his name but I certainly want to believe in what he represents to so many people throughout India and beyond.

For all India's gut-wrenching poverty which these days seems to affront as many as it confronts, there is, too, a richness and completeness to life which can touch the world weary westerner who carries with him only luggage and not the baggage of prejudice and preconception. While the monoculture of the west is disturbingly invasive, millions of Indians, particularly in the heartland, adhere to ancient lore and traditions. In the frenetic, polluted cities the moguls and their minions read anachronism for 'ancient' and seek some accommodation between the god of Mammon and the myriad deities of the Hindu pantheon.

As with everything in India it is not easy to strike the balance. But, of course, nothing is easy in India. This is much of its allure. It is at you all the time—in your face, as a western child of the 1990s might say. It demands you truly consider what you see and feel. It compels you to confront your doubts and fears; expects you to open your heart as well as your mind.

As it is, you are often open-mouthed. For this is the land where a naked holy man will crawl the breadth of the country; the sacred cow has right of passage on roads choked with belching vehicles, where old men with hard bodies swathed in frayed blankets levitate for the benefit of incredulous visitors, where computer boffins compete and often overshadow their contemporaries in the developed world, and politicians of various persuasions boast of the country's nuclear capability.

Life, in all its simplicity and complexity, beauty and ugliness, is lived under the barely averted gaze of others. Certainly there are moments of horror and despair. But there are more compelling moments of wonder and joy. This is a country where your path can be lit as easily by the smile of a toothless leper, a child naked but for a talisman around neck or waist, or the good burghers of megatropolises such as Calcutta and Mumbai.

It is not easy to explain the hold India has on me. Undeniably, there is an empathy of some description and with it has come an easy and comforting acceptance; a sense of being in an appropriate place.

Suffice to say, I've never felt like an outsider in India. Never. And when I'm outside India I think of her and talk about her with a familiarity which is as profound as it may seem incautious if not somewhat high-flown.

Of course, there are many times when I question my right to love so intensely a country which is alternately V.S. Naipaul's *Wounded Civilisation* and an emerging superpower of the new millennium.

But my Indian friends are loving and giving and amused at my almost obsessive need to rationalise, intellectualise my relationship with their land. 'Accept it,' they say. 'It is as it is. It is meant to be. It is God's will. Rejoice in it.'

I once asked a good mate in Chennai whether he could live outside India.

'No, no,' he replied. 'I'm too Indian.'

How I envy him that connection with his land. It may be that I must embark on a more personal journey before I truly understand. Perhaps when there is no longer the need to know, no longer the need to have answered the questions that in all probability cannot be answered, will this true love be revealed as a complete love.

And I sense it is.

BARRY DIVOLA

Sissy Bar

Her name was Emma Montgomery, and she wasn't exactly the girl next door. She was the girl across the street. Waratah Street. Our song was 'When Will I See You Again?' by The Three Degrees. You know? The one that goes, 'When will I see you again? When will our hearts beat together?'

Well, when I say it was our song, it wasn't actually *our* song.

It was more *my* song. But it was *my* song with reference to Emma Montgomery and my intense love for her.

How intense was my love? Well, I started eating mushrooms because of her. Not hallucinogenic mushrooms. I was only a kid at the time. Well, I'm a lot older than that now, and I still haven't eaten hallucinogenic mushrooms … but anyway, I'm talking about your normal garden variety, thrive-on-shit, grow-in-dark-damp-places, do-quite-nicely-with-a-steak style mushrooms.

Here's how it happened.

It was summer. We were on school holidays. We were playing cricket in my driveway. Or possibly sneaky creep-up. That's the game where the person who is 'in' has to sit in a designated spot, and the rest of the gang have to sneak up on them from a distance of fifty yards or so. The person who is 'in' then turns around suddenly and if they catch you moving, then you have to go back to where you started from. This was apparently a lot of fun, as we would spend two or three hours doing it without getting bored at all.

Anyway, it was one of those late summer evenings when the light was sort of fading, but the concrete was still warm from the sun and we all had bare feet and peeling noses from spending too long at the beach. Emma had one of those little button noses, like Sally Field in *The Flying Nun*, but if I get onto that line of thinking I'll be here all day so let me get on with this. So, her little sister came across from the Montgomery house and said, 'Em, Marie wants to know if you want mushrooms with your steak.'

Marie was the Montgomery's housekeeper, who cleaned, cooked and lived with them. Mr Montgomery was divorced. It wasn't until much later, when Marie and Mr Montgomery announced that they were getting married, that I realised Marie was actually a quite attractive young woman who was obviously having an affair with him all this time. Geez, I'm naive.

So, back to the mushrooms.
    Did she want them?
    Yes she did.
    And that was it.
    I wanted mushrooms too.
    Why?
    Because she did.

My family were bland eaters. My father gets aggravated by the taste of onions. He thinks they're too spicy. He also doesn't eat Chinese, Thai or Indian, and he'll eat only very simple Italian dishes. As our surname is Italian, and three of my four grandparents were born in Italy, I always found this a little strange. My personal theory is that he wanted to distance himself from 'wog food' when he was a kid, for fear of being ridiculed. But hey, it's just a theory.

Subsequently, we were a real meat and three veg kind of family. And mum's theory was 'boil the shit out of the vegies until they barely resemble the original plant from whence they came'. So, we got chops with rubbery string beans, mashed potato and mushy peas. Or, for a little variation, cutlets with rubbery string beans, mashed potato and mushy peas. And when she was feeling particularly daring, veal with rubbery string beans, mashed potato and mushy peas. My all-time non-favourite meal—and even the mere mention of it gives me a tickle in the back of my throat, like

I'm about to throw up—was silverside with rubbery string beans, mashed potato and mushy peas. Silverside is the devil's meat. It's kind of like eating a warm, wet washing-up sponge that's been heavily salted. I haven't eaten the stuff since I left home but maybe I should try it again sometime. I once hated broccoli and now I can't get enough of the stuff.

So, back to the mushrooms.

Our family had never had anything as exotic as mushrooms gracing our dinner plates.

'Why, that's crazy, bohemian food! Eat them and you'll become a Communist!' my mother would cry.

Well, she didn't really, but I could tell the sentiment was there.

Emma Montgomery wanted mushrooms. I wanted mushrooms. It was obviously love.

I still love mushrooms. They're the basis of my best pasta dish, and I eat them all the time. I don't think I love Emma Montgomery anymore, and I, er, never got to eat any part of her at all. In fact, I never got to fondle her, see her breasts, kiss her or even hold her hand. And I was in love with her for two years.

This is the way I conducted relationships back in those days—I would worship from afar and mope around and act all casual, but secretly be burning with anticipation, but never let on. I would write her name on my pencil case in block letters, then draw boxes around each letter and diagonal lines across each box, so the name was cleverly disguised to look like a doodle. But I knew it said Emma.

When I think back, I realise that this was to become the template for every relationship I would have with a woman in my life. I'm incredibly slow. I just can't believe that a woman would be interested in me. If they're friendly, well, they're friendly. All that fondling and sex stuff is for other guys to get, not me. I'm the guy with the nice smile and the good personality.

These days that means I'm skinny and bald. Back then it meant I was skinny, had braces and acne. At least I had hair then. But that's another story.

I was also a bit of a nerd. At this stage I was sharing a room with my younger brother. Off our bedroom was a small room which became my study. It never passed on to my brother, or my sister, who was only a year-and-a-half younger than me. Because I was the studious one. I would spend hours doing my homework, not always because I had so much of it, but because I was kind of meticulous and ordered, and even though I was reasonably intelligent, I definitely wasn't super smart. If I was super smart, I would have spent less time in that study and more time exploring Emma Montgomery's wonderful mouth with my tongue. But that pleasure was to fall upon Shane Brady.

The Bradys lived down the end of Waratah Street, in a large house which overlooked the harbour. They had a swimming pool. They had a fantastic stereo system with a Swedish name few of us could pronounce or spell. Yes, they were quite well off. And yes, for a thirteen-year-old in the seventies, to have the surname Brady was a very, very cool thing indeed. Shane once managed to convince my little brother that Greg, Marcia, Peter, Jan, Bobby and Cindy were his cousins, then teased him mercilessly for weeks afterwards. Bastard.

Nah, Shane was a nice enough guy. We just differed on a few things.

Bikes, for instance. You may not think that the pushbike is a big point of difference, but when you're thirteen or fourteen, these sort of things take on Israeli/Palestinian proportions.

For example, one of the defining signs of any teenager in the seventies was the size of your sissy bar. The Freudian ramifications of this are staggering, but let's leave that to those more qualified to interpret these things.

A sissy bar is the curved, chrome bar at the back of the seat of any chopper-style pushbike from that era. They basically came in three sizes—low (raised about three inches, with a kink half way so the last inch was at an angle to the rest of the bike), half (a straight bar that came up to the middle of the rider's back, somewhere just below the middle of the shoulder blades) and full (a tall bar that finished near the rider's head).

Personally, I was a half sissy man. Couldn't see the point in the low sissy. And thought the full sissy was way too ostentatious. I was a middling kinda guy. I wanted to tell the world I was reliable, with the capacity for daring. The half sissy was for me.

I loved my bike. In my whole personal history of birthday presents, this was the one perfect moment. I was turning thirteen, and I knew exactly what I wanted. A blue Malvern Star Dragster with a white seat (with a blue racing stripe), three speed gears with a stubby shift (not a large metallic one with three holes in the shaft) and, of course, the half sissy. I woke up as a thirteen-year-old, looked in the garage and there it was—exactly what was ordered. A man who shunned exotic food and a woman who insisted on cooking silverside every second Thursday night had come through with the goods.

Now Shane, needless to say, was a full sissy kind of guy. He was also not a Malvern Star Dragster kind of guy. He had a Chopper, those lairy machines with large fluorescent tubing for frames and gaudy padded black seats.

Everything about Shane yelled 'I'm a Chopper owner!' He had blond, lank hair that hung to his shoulders. He had already been drunk twice, and thrown up as a result of it once. He had not only tongue pashed two girls but he had touched a girl's breasts and also fingered her. This was the delightful term for manipulating a female's vagina with your digits. I dared not even think of Emma Montgomery in this manner. She was a goddess. I just got a fuzzy feeling thinking about lying down on the driveway next to her and watching the clouds and listening to the sound of her laughing at my jokes. Alas, that never happened, but this was my dream.

So, the fourth form formal came around, and Emma and I were pals, and I didn't want to think about it too much (but I did about eighteen hours a day anyway) but there was just a vague inkling that maybe, possibly, she could ask me to take her.

I mean, we hung out. We'd been friends for a couple of years. I knew she liked me. Not *liked* me liked me, but liked me. I went to a private school in the inner-western suburbs, even though we lived near the beach (my father went there, my uncle taught there, my parents thought the local high school taught kids to be axe-wielding serial killers who sold drugs in their spare time). Emma went to a Catholic school in North Sydney. So occasionally we'd get the same bus home, and of late she'd taken up the habit of saving me a seat when I got on two stops after her. It was a habit I found endearing, loveable, and totally scary at the same time. I also became frozen with inactivity as far as taking this open sign of affection any further. Once again, this was an early indicator of my relationships with women in the future.

I remember exactly how I got the news. I was way too young to remember where I was when JFK was shot, but I do remember man walking on the moon (black and white TV, primary school, I was in love with a tall red-headed girl called Julie), and hearing the news that John Lennon was dead (on the car radio of my first set of wheels, a blue Torana, I was in love with a girl who, funnily enough, looked like Sally Field in *The Flying Nun*). And I remember exactly how I heard that Emma Montgomery was taking Shane Brady to the fourth form formal.

My sister just casually mentioned it when we were having a cup of tea down in the rumpus room one night. In fact, we were listening to *Bat Out Of Hell*. And loving it. There you go, two of the most embarrassing moments in my life captured in one tragic scene. The girl of my dreams is taking someone else to the formal and I'm sitting there with my sister thinking that Meat Loaf is one pretty cool dude.

'Did you hear that Emma's taking Shane to the formal?' my sister said, picking the last shortbread cream out of the jar of Arnott's assorted.

My heart exploded into about a million pieces.

'Nooooooooooooooooooooooooooooo! My God! How could she do this to me? The guy has a full sissy and stupid hair and he … MY GOD … he's touched a girl's breasts and fingered her as well! Emma and I are made for each other! We were meant to go to the formal together, start our first serious romance, let it blossom into a real relationship, then live together dining on mushrooms and listening to our song, which is "When Will I See You Again?", just in case you were wondering!'

My sister didn't react to this outburst at all. She just sat there lifting the top off the shortbread cream and scraping out the filling with her top teeth, tapping her foot to the guitar solo, which I knew was played by Todd Rundgren, because I was a geek who meticulously studied record sleeves while wearing huge white headphones and sitting in a brown velour beanbag on the floor of our rumpus room.

She didn't react because I didn't say anything of the sort. I just had that outburst in my head.

'Really? When is it?' I said quite coolly, I thought, disguising any angst I felt in the most superbly dignified manner.

She wasn't sure when it was.

I could have told her. It was Friday, November 25th. In my diary, under that date, I'd written, in block letters, EMMA'S FORMAL. Then, of course, I'd drawn boxes around each letter and little diagonal lines through those boxes so it just looked like some sort of doodle.

But I knew what it said.

I've never been able to listen to *Bat Out Of Hell* since.

AMY WITTING

The Writing Desk

... it seems well to deserve
　The love we reserve
　　For inanimate things.

　　　　　　　　　　W.H. Auden, *The Railway Engine*

It was the writing desk that sold the room to Emily. She had not expected to find such a piece of furniture in a private house in a country town—an authentic writing desk, its knee-hole flanked by two drawers on each side, the writing surface sheltered by wooden panels which walled its back and sides to create a private working space. A reading lamp, another wonder, was clamped to the left-hand panel.

There was little else to make the room attractive: a large iron bedstead, a combination dressing-table and wardrobe characteristic of any bedroom in any boarding-house, a low cupboard with double doors. There was however a solid straight chair in front of the desk. She had left the rowdy, gabby boarding-house in search of a quiet, private workplace where she could devote her free time to writing her novel. The writing desk seemed to settle the matter.

'What rent are you asking?' she said to the old woman in the doorway. The answer made her gasp.

'I wasn't thinking of board, you know. I should be getting my own meals, of course.'

The old woman seemed not at all perturbed by Emily's reaction. She said placidly, 'Well, you can't go up, but you can come down, that's what I always say.'

'How far are you prepared to come down?'

Not very far, it seemed. She stood firm at forty dollars, which was extortionate. Emily hesitated, but she could not resist the promise of that pool of light and silence which the writing desk offered. Having experience in this matter, she said firmly, 'It is a very high rent, but I shall expect it to cover the cost of electricity. I shall be wanting to work at night.'

The old woman considered this for a moment, apparently with discontent.

'Don't you do your schoolwork at school? They give you time off for that, don't they?'

You truly are an extraordinary old party, thought Emily, as she answered, 'Not enough. I have to bring corrections home. Besides, I am doing a special job.' She knew that it would be unwise to mention novel writing, which would mark her out as an oddity to become the talk of the town. 'I'm writing a thesis. A university thesis. That's why I'm leaving the boarding-house. I want somewhere quiet to work.'

'I wouldn't want anything going on in my house that wasn't respectable.' The old woman seemed to suspect some danger even in a thesis. Perhaps the word 'university' had bad connotations. 'Our name stands high in this town.'

'Not for generosity,' thought Emily. She answered, 'I shan't be doing anything to disgrace you.'

'It'll be payment by the fortnight in advance.'

Emily handed over the eighty dollars, with regret, consoling herself with the thought of that lovely, silent, lighted place which was to be her own.

'I never would have thought of taking a lodger, if it wasn't for the emptiness of the house. If there was anyone, anyone living in the place, even a child ...'

The misery in her voice was moving; it would have affected Emily more deeply if it had not been for the forty dollars paid fortnightly in advance.

'I'll move in, then, on Monday and the rent will be covered until the second Sunday. Monday to Sunday, all right?'

'I suppose so.'

The Writing Desk

The old woman put the notes into a deep pocket of her skirt and the interview was over.

The first shock hit Emily five minutes after she had moved in on Monday. Having put her suitcase on the floor and opened it ready for unpacking, she opened the wardrobe and stared in amazement at the jackets and trousers which crammed the hanging space. She pulled open the drawers and found them filled too with a miscellany of objects: ties, odd socks …

She found her landlady in the kitchen.

'Mrs Britton, you have forgotten to clear out the wardrobe in my room.'

Mrs Britton did not answer at once. Emily now looked at her attentively; till now she had been the fortuitous owner of a room with a writing desk, conspicuous only for her love of money. She was a soft-fleshed, bulky old woman, with white hair dragged back into a knot from a round skull. She had a plump face with neat small features and very pale eyes. At the moment her face wore a look of strange, obtuse calm, like a beached sea-creature pondering new surroundings.

'I did not know you would be wanting that.'

'I did not think I had to mention it. It is generally understood that the rent of a room includes the use of the furniture.'

'Those are Kenny's things. I wouldn't know what to do with Kenny's things.'

'But I must have somewhere to hang up my clothes!' Emily heard and deplored the pleading note in her voice.

'Can't you keep them in your suitcase?'

'No, I can't. Certainly not. I must have the wardrobe cleared.'

'Well, you can't have the cupboard. You can have the wardrobe, I suppose, if you can't do without it, but I can't have you using the cupboard. I need that for storage.' People who required a wardrobe to hang clothes in were clearly monsters of selfishness who needed a firm hand. 'I can't see to it now. I'll have to find some place for Kenny's things. I suppose you can keep your clothes in a suitcase for a day or two.'

This she said with a sneer.

'Oh, yes,' said Emily feebly. 'Just when you have the time.' She expected this remark to elicit a sniff, and so it did.

Why, thought Emily, she's malevolent, a real witch. It's a wonder she stayed civil long enough to collect that rent.

Back in her room and fearing the worst, she pulled open the drawers of the writing desk. Sure enough, the space she intended for her novel outline, her notes, typing paper and carbons, and the chapters as they were completed, was already taken by old account books, worn ink-stained rulers, blunt pencils, eroded rubbers, rubber bands, a set of geometrical instruments. No hope of getting rid of that lot, with permission. She would empty the contents into a couple of cartons and hide them under the bed.

'I'm a rabbit. An absolute wimp. What I ought to do is empty the stuff into cartons, carry them out and say boldly, "What do you want done with this stuff, Mrs Britton? It was in the drawers of my writing-desk."' But she knew that she would not.

She had expected some coolness from the old woman after the disagreement over the wardrobe, but she found her affable and ready to gossip as she showed her the arrangements for cooking and washing. This burner for simmering, that for quick boiling, heat up water on the fuel, electricity too expensive, this accompanied by information about her husband's last illness (cancer right up the fundament), the iniquitous bill for twelve hundred dollars sent by Doctor Burbage to arrive three days after the funeral—'after I had told him again and again to send me a bill by the month and he took no notice. Three days after the funeral. The heartlessness of it!' She spoke of the misdeeds of the Huntleys, who rented from her the house down the road, and had the chip heater roaring every day, so that you could hear it from here, pumping away like a steam engine. 'There'll be a new lining needed for the heater soon. Always needing something, that lot. I'll swear that most of the stuff they complain about is their own doing, or the doing of those children. I'll never let to people with children again, that's certain.'

Mrs Britton indeed covered a lot of ground, showing equal enjoyment in the misdeeds of the Huntleys and the heartlessness of the doctor, among other minor sufferings, as she showed china, cutlery and linens.

'I'll have to keep out of her way,' thought Emily. 'I can't let myself be trapped like this again.'

When Mrs Britton asked her what she meant to cook for her dinner tonight, she was glad to be able to answer that she would be dining out.

The Writing Desk

'I've been invited out to dinner at a friend's house.' And no, I'm not going to tell you by whom, she silently answered the flash of anger which followed the old woman's disconcerted air.

'I hope you won't be coming in late.'

'No. I don't keep late hours, especially when it's school the next day. Ten o'clock at the outside. Can you give me a door key? I wouldn't want to disturb you coming in.' Reluctantly the old woman got up and fetched a large key from a nail behind the kitchen door.

'Surely she isn't going to tell me that I'm not allowed out to dinner,' thought Emily with amusement. For a moment it seemed that the woman was on the point of doing so.

After a cheerful dinner with the deputy and his wife, she walked back to the house and put the key in the door with unease at her strangeness in these surroundings. She opened the door quietly, felt for and found the light switch and pressed it down. That to her surprise required considerable strength. The switch yielded with a loud spanging noise which startled her and might well be enough to waken the old woman.

Damn. Who would expect a light switch to explode with such a crash? She went to her room, turned on the lamp over the writing desk and was comforted at once as it shone down on what was to be her private working space.

Ready for bed, and back in the hall, she tried to work the switch more gently, out of respect for the old woman's sleep, but there was no help for it. The switch resisted, then yielded with the same loud spang as before. Maybe she is used to it, she thought, yawning. She set her alarm clock, put out her light and fell asleep.

A worse shock came next afternoon, when she set up her typewriter on the desk, fed in the first page of her novel and set to work. It was a moment of special joy, but it did not last long. The old woman rushed into the room, looking wild-eyed, hands covering her ears, crying, 'Stop it! I can't have that noise! I won't have that terrible noise in the house! It goes right through my head! As if the noise you made coming in last night wasn't bad enough. I can't put up with this. I can't stand that noise. It's giving me a terrible headache.'

Emily might have known that it was all too good to be true. That lovely well of light and silence the desk had promised could not be for her.

'I'm very sorry. I did take it for granted that I should be able to type. If I can't type, then I can't stay. I'll stay for the fortnight, of course, because I have paid the rent, but meanwhile I'll look for something else.'

She said later, as she described the scene to her friend Miriam, 'If ever you saw two eyes convert into dollar signs before your own …' Mrs Britton had taken her hands from her ears. Her headache appeared to have abated. She stood hesitating. Emily seized the advantage.

'I'll get a piece of felt to put under the typewriter. That will cut the noise a lot. And I'll keep my door shut. If at the end of the fortnight you find you can't bear it, then I'll leave. What about that?'

'I suppose it's worth trying. If you must.'

Emily gave up typing for the afternoon, for the lack of the felt baffle. She applied herself to cleaning out two drawers of the desk and boldly stacked the contents in the corner of the room, ready to be packed into a carton. The old woman would certainly investigate and find them tomorrow. Emily thought she would not care to mention the matter.

Nothing more was said about the typing. Perhaps the noise, dulled by the layer of felt and the wooden panels, did not reach the old woman, whose habitat was the kitchen. Perhaps, on the other hand, she was daunted by the fear of losing the rent. Emily finished her first chapter, so long planned and written in longhand, and at the weekend, started on the next. On reflection, she put the top copy of the first chapter into a folder and took it to her friend Miriam, the only inhabitant of the town who knew of her serious literary ambitions. She handed her the folder, saying, 'Do me a favour, will you? Look after the top copy of my novel for me. I just don't trust my landlady. Silly of me, but I'd be happier if you looked after it for me.'

'I'd love to. May I read it?'

'Of course you may. You and Mrs Britton. I'm dead certain that as soon as I leave for school she gets into my room to find out what I'm doing. I can stand that. I haven't much choice. But … I don't know. Just look after it for me. And I hope you will read it. I do want to know what you think of it, but don't tell me till it's finished.'

Miriam took the folder.

'I'll look after it for you. I wouldn't trust her either. She's the meanest old snake in town. All her children have cleared out, and no wonder that poor Stella ran off with a man of seventy. Mrs Wingrove next door said the old woman never let up on the poor girl, and they used to hear her crying. But a man of seventy! And now she has a baby girl. Imagine, she'll have a husband over eighty and a child under ten—what a future! But better than life with mum.'

'She does her own share of crying. If you try to argue with her and she can't get her own way, she absolutely breaks down, sobs like an infant. Like over the noise I made coming in that first night. The light switch makes an incredible spanging noise, enough to wake the dead, I agree. So I disturbed her sleep. She held on to her grievance till the next time I went out, then she said, she couldn't stand having her sleep disturbed by noise at night and she hoped I'd be more careful in the future. I thought, "Oh hell, the light switch!" and I said, very reasonably, I thought, that I could not understand why anyone so sensitive to noise should have light switches that went off like a bomb, and she started to cry. "The boys fixed them like that, for safety." Insoluble problem. You want the safety, you take the noise. Though really, I'm buying a torch to get around with at night. No point in making any trouble.'

'Why on earth did you go there? I could have warned you.'

'It's only till I finish the book. I've won the point about typing. That's the main thing. She did try to stop it.' Emily described the scene and made the remark about eyes which turned into dollar signs.

'It's lucky I made an absolute point that forty-dollar rent would have to cover the use of electricity, because I meant to work at night. Of course I don't type at night, but I'm doing the first draft by hand, and I leave my corrections till after dinner. So there's plenty to do.'

She did not mention the private place, the little lighted room formed by the lamp and the wings and back of the writing desk. Nomads find homes in strange places.

It was lucky indeed that Emily had insisted that the forty-dollar rent covered the use of electricity. She discovered in the following weeks that there were many things it did not cover: toilet paper (Sorry, I'll buy a roll.), washing-up liquid, (Sorry, I'll get myself a bottle tomorrow and you can use some of mine.), laundry soap (Sorry, I just didn't think. I won't do it again.), floor polish (Okay, I'll get my own.), sinful and extravagant use of the chip heater for a daily bath (It's a wonder what some people do to get so dirty.). That one Emily preferred to ignore, since she had no intention of giving up the daily bath.

'She hasn't thought of wear and tear on the broom yet,' said Emily to Miriam. She was laughing, for she had decided to classify Mrs Britton as a comic character.

'I don't know how you put up with it. I'd love to have you here, you know, but Graham says it isn't possible for a doctor to take in lodgers. He say it's a confession of failure. Well, why doesn't he admit he's a failure and take a salaried job in the city? He says it's my fault, because I don't socialise, but Mary Burbage is no angel and Burbage's practice goes along all right. But that's Graham, always someone else's fault, never his own.'

Emily, who did not wish to be exposed every day to Miriam's bitter unhappiness, said that she could see Graham's point of view, 'in a place like this, where everyone is out to make the worst of anything.'

'Besides, it really suits me. If she wasn't so poisonous, I might feel I had to socialise. As it is, it's minimal exposure. Well, I do see her at breakfast, and then I get a few remarks about the dirty habits of those who find it necessary to bathe every day, but I let that pass in silence and get on with my cornflakes. And I don't cook dinner, just have cold cuts and salad. I don't eat till seven o'clock and by then she's out of the kitchen. I've had a few remarks about eating at a reasonable hour, and I point out in a reasonable tone that I like to do my typing at a time when I know it won't disturb her.

'So I type from five to seven, then I eat and wash up, then correct essays and maybe begin a new chapter. I don't care for anything, so long as I finish the book. I'm fired up. I've been thinking about it, planning it for so long and never had the chance, never had a place where I could sit and work and know I won't be interrupted. Two hours a day and most of Saturday, when I've done my washing and cleaning, and just about all of Sunday. You can't imagine what it means to me.'

'Oh, I think I can.'

'Yes. I know you do. I'd put up with anything, just for the chance to write in peace.'

'It's a wonderful book. I finish one chapter and I can't wait to get the next one.'

'I hope some publisher agrees with you.'

'Oh, they will! They must!'

'Well, it's worth putting up with the old lady and that dreadful rent I can't afford, just to have this one chance.'

'Have another cup of coffee.'

'No. I'd better be getting back, or there'll be remarks at breakfast about people who come in at all hours without consideration for the sleep of others.'

'And this using a torch! You shouldn't have paid any attention to her moaning about the light switches!'

'I think she lies awake, waiting to see if I do anything to wake her up. Don't worry. I'm bearing up. Honestly, it's a bit of a laugh.'

'When do I get the next chapter?'

'Next Friday night, if you'll be home.'

'Sure. I'd love to see you.'

When Emily arrived on Friday evening with the new chapter, she found Miriam in distress.

'I have to talk to you. Thank God, Graham's out visiting a patient. I don't want him in on this.'

'What's the matter?'

'Oh, that Rhoda Britton! I was at the Burbages' on Tuesday afternoon, playing bridge. It was fundraising for the Red Cross, more people there than usual, not all friends of Mary's. Otherwise the beastly woman wouldn't have been there. Mary would never have invited her. She was telling the world what a bad character you were, how poor Auntie was at her house crying about it. She'd taken a lodger in for the company after Uncle Fred died and you just ignored her. I was so furious, I said, "Took her in for company, indeed! Took her in for forty dollars a week, you mean. Charging an exorbitant rent and doing nothing for her. If she wanted company, she should have halved the rent and offered a bit of service." I don't believe Rhoda knew about the rent, and it shocked her. It shocked everyone. Jane Croft said, "Why, you could get a self-contained flat for that." I said, "And if you did let a self-contained flat, would you expect the tenant to come and keep you company in the evenings?" Rhoda didn't know what to say. I suppose I should have left it at that, but I couldn't help myself. I said, "If your aunt had been looking for company, perhaps she should have chosen someone a little more on her own intellectual level."'

And there went Graham's practice again, thought Emily. Miriam did not know where to stop.

'She'd have said it anyhow. What she said. Of course I'd got under her skin. She isn't exactly proud of Auntie. And said it somewhere where I wasn't there to argue.'

'Miriam, what did she say?'

Miriam braced herself.

'She said you might be doing better than staying in your room day and night drinking.'

'*What!*'

'Yes. That's what I said. I said you didn't drink. She said, "Oh, yes she does. Auntie has seen the bottles." Emily, I know there's no truth in it.'

'There's an atom of truth in it. I sometimes drink a glass of sherry at night. It puts me to sleep. A bottle of sherry lasts more than a fortnight. Of course she's seen bottles, two maybe in eight weeks.'

'If a thing like this gets around in a town like this, your life won't be worth living.'

'It would get around the school, that's the problem.' Emily was engulfed in depression. 'I thought I could put up with anything, to get the book finished, but I can't let this pass. I'll have to tackle her and make her retract. So she'll put me out. No help for it. She's got to give me notice. I won't budge till the end of term, that's three weeks. There are the term papers to mark. But I won't give up work on my book if I have to sit up all night. Damn the old wretch and her electricity bill.'

'Can't you work in the holidays?'

Emily shook her head. 'I'll be staying with Diana. If she knows about the novel, she'll never let me help out with the kids. And with two toddlers and a baby, she needs all the help she can get.'

'It seems to me that you could do with a break.'

'My sister Diana is about the closest person to me on earth. I don't grudge it, I assure you. She'll be there for me if I need her. Meanwhile, I have to think how to handle the old party.'

Next morning, carrying writing pad, envelopes and pen, and armed with resolution, Emily advanced on the enemy in the kitchen.

'Mrs Britton, did you give your niece Rhoda reason to understand that I drink to excess?'

'She's not my niece, she's my second cousin!'

'Did you give your second cousin reason to understand that I drink to excess?'

The old woman was flustered but defiant. 'I didn't say anything about excess!'

Emily sat down opposite her and prepared for a long struggle.

'And I didn't say "said". I said "give to understand". If you say that a person drinks, the implication is that she drinks to excess. That is certainly how Rhoda Britton understood it and communicated her opinion to a number of people at Mrs Burbage's house last Tuesday. Her words were that I sat in my room all day drinking, and that you had seen the bottles. Did you think to tell her how many bottles you had seen?'

'A young woman like you shouldn't be drinking alcohol at all.'

'I have my own ideas about what people should and should not do. We can discuss that some other time. How many bottles?'

The old woman withdrew into silent resentment.

'How many bottles?'

'How would I know?'

'Too many to count, was it? That was the impression your relative gave the company. I'll tell you how many. Two. Two empty sherry bottles in eight weeks. Do you call that heavy drinking?'

'I suppose not.'

Emily put the pad and the pen on the table in front of her. 'Now you are to write to your relative. You are to tell her that you did not mean to give the impression that I drank to excess, that in the eight weeks I have lived in your house you have seen only two empty sherry bottles in the bin and have no reason to suppose that I spend my time in my room drinking. I want you to do this now.'

'Why should I?'

'Because if she doesn't get a letter from you, she'll be getting one from Frank Brown, the solicitor, and so will you. You'll both be facing a charge of slander.'

The word 'slander' stood like a solid object in the old woman's path. She eyed it with caution.

'I don't mind putting Rhoda right. She had no right to repeat what I told her in confidence.'

'What you had no right to say in the first place.' With every statement Emily's voice grew firmer. 'Start writing, please. And start with the date. "Dear Rhoda, it has come to my attention that last Tuesday …"' I am enjoying this, thought Emily. Bullying people is fun. It could get to be a habit. I must remember that.

She dictated, the old woman wrote. She stopped over the word 'implication'.

'Rhoda will know I never wrote that.'

'I am sure that Rhoda will understand the situation perfectly. Go on, please. "In the eight weeks she has lodged in my house, she has …"'

'I can't stand this! I can't stand this!' Tears of aggrieved and bullied childhood rolled down the old woman's face.

'I can't help it. If the story gets to the school that I am a secret drinker, then my career as well as my reputation will be ruined. I have to protect myself against slander. Go on writing, please.' Her voice was gentler, for the old woman's misery was genuine. Emily told herself firmly that it did not spring from remorse.

They finished the letter. 'Now I am going to type a copy of this, and I want you to sign and date them both. If Rhoda does not do as you've said, and speak to Mrs Burbage, then I'll have to make sure that she gets the information.'

She was glad to escape from the scene of the old woman's destruction and her own deterioration.

She brought back the letter and the copy.

'Now sign the copy, please, and date your signature.'

As the old woman wrote, she cried out in a moaning voice, mournful as a dirge.

'If you knew what it was like, living with someone who doesn't have a word to throw you from morning till night. If I get "Good morning" and "Good afternoon" from you, it's as much as I'll ever get. You'd give more thought to a dog than you give to me. And no consideration, not a thought for my sleep, coming in at all hours …'

'I don't use those light switches. I use a torch.'

'You have a particularly heavy tread.'

'Well, thank you for letting me know. Now, if you address the envelope, I'll post it.' She was thinking with horror, 'She wanted love. She wanted me to love her. That poor, mean-tongued, avaricious creature. She wants love.'

'I can't even look for a word over the dinner table. Eating that nasty cold stuff at any hour, like a gypsy.'

'My diet is healthy and adequate. I think that you have expected too much of a lodger.'

'I'd have been ready to cook you a bit of dinner, if you'd asked.'

'I wouldn't want to put you to the trouble. Come on, address the envelope and we'll forget all about it. I'll never use that copy unless I really have to. You just have a word with Rhoda and tell her she has to kill the story, that's all.'

Her voice was almost as sad as the old woman's, weighed as it was with the burden of all the unloveable people who yearned for love. If she could not give love, she would at least give forgiveness.

'I can't understand,' said Emily to Miriam, 'why she has taken it so quietly.'

A week had passed and the notice of dismissal had not come.

'Rhoda hasn't taken it quietly. She gave me a poisonous look at the last Red Cross committee meeting. The old lady is probably frightened.'

'It's more than that,' said Emily. 'She looks somehow … thoughtful. Subdued, but—I would have expected her to be more resentful.'

'You had to do it, you know,' said Miriam firmly.

'Oh yes, I know.' *But I shouldn't have enjoyed it.* She felt nauseous, remembering the pleasure she had felt in watching the old woman write at her dictation. Once or twice she had had to impose her will on refractory children, though not often. She was lucky in that; she could not herself explain why a noisy class would become quiet when she entered the room. When other teachers asked for the secret, she would answer, 'I don't know. I suppose I just expect it.' She could not imagine taking pleasure in dominating and humiliating a child. If it had to be done, she could do it, but to enjoy it … the thought was disgusting. *I shall never seek power over another human being again, so long as I live.*

Aloud, she said, 'Well, it doesn't look as if she's going to put me out. That's the main thing. I'll know by the end of the term, when I pay for the fortnight's rent for the holidays. If she doesn't tell me to pack my bags then, I'll know that she's decided to swallow it.'

'It's a bore having to pay when you're away.'

'That's the big drawback about renting, but it means I can leave my things. Don't have to clear the room out. That's something.'

'I'll store your stuff for you, love, if she does throw you out.'

On the last day of term, Emily handed eighty dollars to Mrs Britton saying, 'I'll be off tomorrow morning and I'll be back on Sunday fortnight. Probably in the morning. I'll take the night train.' The old woman did hesitate for a moment. Now was the moment to say, 'I don't want you to come back.' The sight of the money must have been too persuasive. She took the money without a word. One would wonder, thought Emily, with an inward grin, at what some people are prepared to swallow for forty dollars a week.

For the first week of the vacation, Emily managed to put the novel out of her mind. At the first sight of her younger sister, thin, wan and prematurely ageing, she had exclaimed, 'Di, you look terrible!'

'The baby's sleep pattern isn't established yet. I haven't been getting much sleep. Peter does help at the weekends,' she said, forestalling criticism of her husband, which Emily might entertain, though she would not express it. 'He has to have his sleep during the week, so he wears earplugs and I cope. Derek and Edgar keep me going during the day, so there you are. It's a bad spell.'

'I'll take the boys over. You look after the baby. You sleep when he sleeps. You have to get some rest.'

Diana nodded, saying, 'It's not much of a holiday for you but ... I'd be grateful.' The manner which imposed discipline on the rowdy classes had no effect on four-year-old Derek and two-year-old Edgar. Emily ran, caught, washed, fed and entertained, balancing on a knife-edge between affection and exasperation. The undoubted charm of the human infant was, she decided, a survival mechanism. Without it, one would certainly throw them out of a high window onto their fragile skulls.

Diana, meanwhile, ate breakfast in bed and went back to sleep till the baby cried for its ten o'clock feed. She relaxed. Peace and a little colour came back to her face; observing the change, Emily thought of her efforts as rewarded.

Peter also balanced on a knife-edge between gratitude and resentment. The young women were closely bound in affection, having been allies in the difficult household of their father's second marriage. Peter did not care for that closeness; most particularly, he did not want Emily to regard his house as her home. This attitude, never expressed in words, was however clear to Emily. At the weekend the cool wind of courtesy blew. Emily thought, 'All the home I have in this world is made up of a writing desk, a reading lamp and a typewriter.' The thought started a concentrated longing for that small private place.

When she took breakfast to Diana on Monday, she sat on the bed, saying, 'Love, I've got something to tell you. Better take my chance while the kids are watching *Play School*.' She laughed at the sudden attentiveness in Diana's face.

'No. I have not met Mr Right. Forget him. I'm writing a novel.'

'Oh, Em!' Diana's start of delight jiggled the breakfast tray and spilled coffee into the saucer. 'That's wonderful. I've always known you should do more with your life, you just have it in you to be something special. You're not just anybody. This is it.'

'I've proved nothing yet. What I want to say is, I'd like to go back early. You are looking better. A couple of days should set you up.'

'Peter's getting a student to help for two hours after school. That's crisis time, when I'm trying to feed the boys and get them ready for bed, and Jeremy is very unsettled. It is going to make all the difference.'

'How to repel invaders,' thought Emily.

'It's your doing,' said Diana, answering the unspoken thought. 'When he saw how worried you were, and ready to give up your holiday. I truly am so grateful!'

Emily answered only with a smile.

'It's all right, then, if I leave on Wednesday? But you have to make the most of me until then. I'll get back to the boys now. Don't worry about the tray, I'll get it later.'

'Give me a hug.'

Emily obliged and went downstairs to resume her duties.

In the night train she planned her next chapter and wrote the outline and certain pithy expressions which must not be forgotten, before she got into the sleeper—a necessary expense, rather than a luxury, after ten days of looking after her nephews. She slept soundly and woke happy, thinking of duty done and Diana restored, relishing her freedom and ready for work. She took a taxi—or rather, the taxi took her—to Mrs Britton's house.

There was a car in the drive. 'Early in the morning for entertaining,' thought Emily, but she was pleased that the old woman had a visitor. She could go straight to her room without announcing her arrival.

The bed was unmade, a slept-in bed, which told the whole story with shocking suddenness. She looked about. Her typewriter was not on her desk. Instead there were a stranger's brush, comb and mirror, face powder, face cream—evidence enough of settled occupancy.

She sped to the kitchen, where Mrs Britton sat with another woman at the breakfast table. It was not a moment for introductions. Emily fixed her eye on Mrs Britton and shrilled in fury, 'Who has been sleeping in my room?' Later, she thought that she could have been trying out for the part of Father Bear in the Christmas pantomime, but at the moment fury ruled.

Mrs Britton answered in indignation, 'You're not supposed to be back till Sunday.'

'That has nothing to do with you. While I pay rent for the room, nobody else has the right to use it.' Her voice rose to a shout. 'I demand an explanation.'

A wail of fright from a small child startled her. She looked at the third person present, a youngish woman with a worn, gentle countenance which was in itself a reproach. Emily now saw that she was holding a baby girl on her knee. The little girl was whimpering as she stared at Emily.

'I didn't mean to frighten the child, I'm sorry. But this must not happen again.'

'It's my house, I suppose.'

'If you had wanted to use the room, you should have asked my permission. Well, I should have given permission, but I shouldn't have been paying rent for the room while someone else was occupying it.'

'I didn't ask you for the rent. You gave it to me.'

'Oh, come off it. Did you think it was a present?'

'Kept your things there, didn't we? Nothing's come to any harm. It's not like renting.'

'If it comes to charging for storage, perhaps I should be charging storage, too, for the cupboard you have crammed with your stuff in my room. You can just get your stuff out of there.' Emily's tone was dulcet, out of consideration for the baby. She perceived that the scene was becoming comic.

Mrs Britton stiffened, set her lips and communed with some inward presence who understood right behaviour.

The young woman spoke. Her voice was as gentle and as worn as her face.

'Miss Balfour is right, mother. You should not have taken the rent and I think you ought to give it back.' As she made this audacious suggestion, her voice quavered.

Her mother turned on her.

'Don't you use that tone with me!' The tone had been mild to the point of extinction, but by objecting to the tone, Mrs Britton could of course avoid discussion of the meaning. 'Lucky I'm prepared to have you in my house at all, after you've made me a laughing stock, running off with your old Romeo. Dirty old man!'

The baby girl who had been frightened by the anger in Emily's voice appeared to be soothed by her grandmother's tirade. These must be the sounds of home, too familiar to be threatening, and this must be the daughter Stella.

'Jack is a good man, a good, kind man, and we are happy together. And I will not have you speaking ill of her father in front of Philippa.' With this protest the young woman seemed to have reached the limit of her courage. Emily sensed that she had been using physical strength to force out every word.

'Father indeed. Great-grandfather, more like!'

Any pity Emily might have felt for Mrs Britton was extinguished. She said, 'Mrs Britton, will you please listen to me? You do not seem to understand anything about the law. You have taken money under false pretences, and that is called fraud. I cannot take action against you, because I don't have enough evidence that you took the money.' The old woman's expression relaxed. There, thought Emily, went her last chance of getting her money back. 'But in the future you will sign a dated receipt for every cent I pay you. Then, if there is any more fraudulent conduct on your part,

I shall have evidence and I shall know what to do.' After this pompous speech, which she knew to be perilously close to the ridiculous, she waited for the woman to say, 'Don't bother. You can pack your things and get out.' That seemed to be the only possible answer. The old woman however chose not to answer at all, except with the all-purpose sneer. It was the daughter who bowed her head under the weight of the humiliation and stared scarlet-faced at the tablecloth.

Stella looked up at length and said, 'I'll drive out and spend a few days with Gwen and Harry', got up and carried the baby into the invaded room. Emily followed. Stella had set the child on the floor and was gathering up her possessions from the desk and putting them into a travel bag.

'You would have been welcome to stay as my guest,' said Emily, 'if I had been asked. It was a shock, coming in and finding the room … really, I am sorry. I know you did not understand the situation.'

Stella said indifferently, 'I'll change the sheets.'

It was no use. There had been too many tirades, too many humiliations. Emily could hope only that Jack was indeed a good man who had brought the poor woman some happiness.

'Where is my typewriter, please?' she asked diffidently.

Stella winced before she answered, 'On the top shelf of the linen press. I'll fetch it.'

'I'll go. I'll get the sheets.'

Stella accepted the offer of help with the same indifference. She nodded and began to take clothes out of the wardrobe. It was clear that her only thought was to get out of the house as soon as possible.

It was done, the room cleared of strange possessions, the typewriter back in its place, order restored. Stella had responded with a silent nod to Emily's farewell and departed. Emily sat down at the desk and waited for her hands to stop shaking. She typed. 'The qrick brown foz fumped … the qr …' How could any woman love money so much, more than dignity, more than self-respect, more than … It wasn't need, according to Miriam. Mrs Britton was a rich woman.

It's nothing to do with me, thought Emily firmly. She got the notes for the next chapter out of her travel bag, the world of her novel closed round her and she began to type.

THE WRITING DESK

She bought a receipt book. When on Sunday she paid for the rent she presented the receipt book and a pen and watched Mrs Britton fill in the receipt—date, amount and signature. After all, it was a normal procedure, wasn't it? She should have done this in the first place.

'How did she take it?' asked Miriam, who had listened with delight to Emily's account of the confrontation and the history of the receipt book.

'Oh, no fuss. She didn't seem to mind. In her place, I should be seething. I'll never know why she didn't tell me to leave after the row.'

'With her standards, she probably took it for normal conversation.'

It was Emily who minded. Whenever she presented the receipt book with her rent, she remembered how she had stood over the old woman, dictating the letter to Rhoda. The satisfaction she had felt then became uglier in her memory; she applied to it words like 'gloating' and 'glee'. That satisfaction had been followed by a nauseous reaction; whenever she watched the old woman sign the receipt, that nausea returned.

She came back from school one day to find the cupboard in her room open and empty. When she told Miriam this, she said, 'I wish I could get out. If it weren't for the novel ...'

'What's the matter with you? Why aren't you pleased? She should have cleaned out the cupboard in the first place.'

'I don't want the wretched cupboard. I don't want her trying to please me, that's all. Ever since she started signing those receipts, she's been like a different person. No complaints about the bath heater, no complaints about noise.'

'You've got her frightened. She's always dominated everyone in that house, the old man too. He was a sour old cuss, but he never stood up to her. Now you come talking about slander, talking about fraud, letters from solicitors, receipts. Now she knows there's an authority bigger than she is, and she doesn't know quite how big it is. So she's wary.'

Emily nodded.

'I did say something about using my room for storage. She might think there's some law against that. But it's not just that. She's almost friendly. Offered me a cup of tea the other day. You'd think she was glad to meet someone who stood up to her.'

'Isn't that all to the good?'

'As if she was glad to be stopped. You meet children like that sometimes, really bad children, who hate and despise you because you don't know how to stop them.'

'Why does it worry you?'

'Bullies create toadies, but toadies create bullies. Every time I watch her sign a receipt, I feel more and more of a bully.'

'You are entitled to defend your interests.'

'At what point does defence become aggression? The big international question. Power over another person I simply don't want.'

'It's not a very great power, is it?'

'All power corrupts, and all corruption is absolute. I don't think that woman is capable of feeling shame, and she has a wonderful knack of making you feel it for her. I noticed that with the unfortunate daughter, who couldn't be blamed for the situation, crimson with shame and misery over her mother's behaviour.'

'But that's different. You do feel like that when your parents or your children disgrace themselves. You identify. But not with a landlady. It seems odd to me, that you can't simply pay your rent and do your work and leave it at that. Why do you have to involve yourself at all?'

'Oh, yes. Why does one? That's the mystery. Well, it won't be long now. As soon as I finish the book … well, it'll be nearly the end of term and that will be the end of it. No more of Mrs Britton, thank goodness.'

As Emily put together the pages of the final chapter and secured them with a paperclip, she felt the chill of homelessness take possession as it always did at the end of the year, stronger this time than usual. She stroked the writing surface of the desk, thinking, 'You've served your turn, and now goodbye.' Her sense of loss was acute and startling. She closed her eyes over ridiculous tears. Well, after all, some quite grown-up people go gaga over teddy bears. No, not a teddy bear. More like a ship. It was quite respectable to cry over a ship. She patted the right-hand panel, thinking, 'Some day, if I can write books that sell, I shall have a place of my own, and in it there will be a desk just like you.' Then she wiped away the two tears with a finger and set off to take the chapter to Miriam.

As soon as she arrived at the house, Miriam seized the pages, saying,

'I can't wait. I'm going to read this straight away. You go and make yourself a cup of coffee.'

Emily drank coffee, looked at a magazine, fidgeted and waited, till Miriam looked up, laughing.

'You've sprung a surprise. But when I look back, yes. I shouldn't be so surprised. It's all there. Emily, it's marvellous. You must have a wonderful sense of achievement.'

'Well, yes. At finishing it at all. Whether it's any good … that's for others to say. I hope you are right. But I feel sad. It's sort of a safe house, writing a novel. You're in your own little world and you control it and can shut out everything else. So I feel kind of homeless. And I haven't made any arrangements for the holidays. So in practical terms, I am homeless.'

'How did it happen, Emily? It seems so dreadful, to have no home.'

'Dad left the house to Delia. Right and proper, she was his wife. To Dad it was the family home and we were all one family. He never knew how bad things were between Di and me, and Delia and her kids. I don't think he ever dreamed that Delia would get rid of us.'

'His own children!'

'I wouldn't want to live there anyhow. I have a corner of the basement where I keep possessions in a tea chest and an old trunk, and I go there when I want something. I suppose I could have a bed there if I were desperate, but it would be a last resort. It's all right. I'll have Christmas with Peter and Di and the children. That's acceptable. And then I'll find something. Have to find something for next year too. Maybe I'll get a move.'

'Oh, Emily, no! If you go, there'll be nobody in this bloody town to talk to.'

'I'd miss you, too. But teachers don't get much choice, you know.'

Emily paid the last fortnight's rent and collected the last receipt.

'I shan't be wanting the room next year, Mrs Britton. I'll take all my things and leave the room free for a new tenant.'

It took Mrs Britton more than a moment to put a decent face on astonishment and dismay.

'That's a pity. Just when we were getting into each other's ways.'

Nikki Gemmell

My Name is Disturbance

I could crush diamonds and drink them, I could row into the middle of a lake and dive deep into the water with an anchor around my neck, I could let the bubbles close over me or the fragments grind into me.

That is what you were told.

Or I could just go.

It was decided at my high window, as I contemplated stepping into a star-stained sky. A glass of red wine was dragging me into sleep but I turned back to my desk and took up the pen—the ink one, your gift—and the letter to you was finally done. A day later I was skimming above clouds that stretched to the horizon like an ocean of ice. I was on a plane to the rest of my life and you were not to be told where.

I was leaving the land where the light roars and the sea hurts.

> *Exile is not a word*
> *It is a sound*
> *The rending of skin.*
>
> Peter Woods

The city I came to had parks that were reluctant. In those first few weeks I walked around and around the perimeter of their empty green, disbelieving, trying to find a way in. But the gates were locked and the fence iron was spiked and couldn't be scaled.

The city I came to had stone that was harder and sharper and blonder and smoother than the honey-grainy, soft Sydney sandstone I had left. The new stone was fine and cold to the touch and it stained the tips of my fingers black.

The city I came to had swimming pool water that had the thickness of many bodies in it. Hair tangles danced like soft seaweed on the bottom of the pools, ghostly bandaids shimmied to the water's rhythm—lifting and settling, lifting and settling—and I swam my slow freestyle and felt like an Amazon, for everyone else was doing dogpaddle.

The city I came to didn't have stars. 'It is the light pollution,' my Pakistani newsagent explained to me, 'all of the brightness has bled away the sky.' You wouldn't have stood for a bled away sky. As I wouldn't have, once.

The city I came to was London.

I left on the marriage cusp, I ran far with my wealth and my crime. I was twenty-five—the physical prime, so it's said, of a woman's life. I am forty-two now and there is still a girlishness to my small breasts. They are the breasts of a young woman. I showed them off to my best friend from school the last time she visited. 'Yes, but what price has been paid for them?' I saw flit in her eyes.

Antonio is beside me now, asleep. His body thuds into mine as if he is trying to draw the warmth from my skin. He is demonstrative in slumber. His limbs and his torso cling to me and clamp me down. On these deep winter nights I make him warm his fingers for five minutes on the hot water bottle before he is allowed to touch my skin.

It is cold, so cold and I have never settled into it. Each winter the chill seeps into my bones and lodges there, as persistent as mould.

Antonio and I will not last beyond the Spring together. I will see to it.

After seventeen years these things will not fade.

At night we used to fold our bodies into each other's like a jigsaw. When you kissed my ears you told me they blushed. When you trickled your hands over the back of my neck it was like cool water on a hot summer's day. When we were far from our city at night you would gently tug at my ponytail, guiding my face to the complexity of the sky. When I woke from sleep you would sometimes be curled around me, your arm threaded under mine and your hand softly balled in my groin. When I caught sight of you from a distance, if I hadn't seen you for a while, I would get a tremor in my bowels deep inside me, like the beginning signal of an orgasm. I would be hurting with tenderness at the sight of you.

These things do not fade.

On the first Sunday after my arrival in this land I took a train to a strange, stony beach and I breathed in the sea. The waves were tight and small and demure, they folded too neatly, and the ocean was the colour of cold, milky tea. It was summer in England and the skin of the people didn't suit it. There were young boys with wetsuits on in the water, thermoses of tea, matchstick mats under towels on the stones. There were Sunday couples doing what Sunday couples do the world over and family groups and pensioners and I felt a vast, swamping loneliness within it all.

I didn't have the courage to ring you and I didn't have the courage to return.

Because ten days earlier my bewildered family had first heard of my plan. I had asked them to understand my choice, to try not to judge or condemn, to acknowledge the courage in risk.

Because for six months I had been asking myself, so tentatively and wondrously at first, what is the decision I can make that is magnificent enough to give meaning to my life?

I am forty-two and my breasts are still young. After you, I never shared my life with anyone. My mother tells me you never had children either.

Exile is not a word
It is a shaving against
A photograph, not a mirror.

Peter Woods

It has taken me so long to judge that my crime was so wrong.

I craved weather in the city I came to. The rain in London was weak, there was no weight in it. I wanted wind and push and bash and wet, I wanted rain like at home that vanished clothes in three seconds, I wanted wet that was drenching and triumphant and complete. But the weather in London didn't reach the shy window of that first bedsit I found, a room at the bottom of a tall alley. I had to lean my body far out the window and twist my head until it hurt to catch the sky.

I craved the tall blue, stretched land, hurting light.

When I left you I was like a small wooden boat whose anchor had snapped in choppy waters, I was lurching and dipping and almost capsizing *but I was free*. Exile, I had decided, was to be my handicap. I knew no-one in this country or no-one I wanted to seek out, I had no mentor, no confidante, no crutch. I chose anonymity and all its freedoms, the thrill of freefall, no net. And I prayed for the courage of total surrender.

This is not my country.

This country is grapes in winter and nipples in newspapers, carpets in bathrooms and closed-over pools. 'Oh, a colonial,' I was told when my vowels were heard. The new Australians I met told me it was a rare thing to be invited into an Englishman's home. 'They don't like us,' I was told, 'It's hard work getting close to them.' 'We irritate them, our accent isn't liked.' But my writing sucked the marrow from adversity. And I could never write in the molasses happiness that we had in Sydney, it was all too distractingly good. It scattered my focus and my thinking, my hunger.

This is not my country. My father's mother was born here and I have no affinity for this land. Two generations is all it has taken to wipe the slate clean. It is not under my skin, it is not fiercely held in my heart, and yet for seventeen years I have stayed.

You told me once that the word enthusiasm came from the Greek, *enthusios*, meaning spark of God, and I saw that in you and I loved you for it and then despaired at its diminishing. Your spirit was leaking towards the end. You wanted children. A wife.

It all distilled the night I strode out after a stupid argument about a broken teacup. There was the horrible, exhilarating hit of it as I walked the glary, jangly inner city streets, drinking in the faces of the people around me, there was the knowing that I was more vivid and alive and experiencing and seeing. Alone.

My Name is Disturbance

· · ·

When I moved in with you the writing stopped. I wavered with you, I went soft.

> *How I regret now that perpetual emotional dependence on the man I love has killed all my other talents—my energy too: and I had such a lot of that once.*
> Sofia Tolstoy, *Diary*, December 1890

On my first birthday in exile my grandmother posted me a card with nothing written on it. She remembered she had done this and rang me an hour after sending it. 'That's the end of me then,' her voice zoomed with laughter. She was eighty-nine. She had fallen pregnant with my father in 1916 and her lover then had to leave for the front. He promised to marry her when he came home. He was killed in action and she never touched another man. She moved to Australia to start a new life.

The English summer shut itself down and the first winter came, as abrupt as a rollerdoor slamming down on the warmth. I began foolishly counting days: fifteen since sun, fifteen since a shadow. I was rattled, deeply, with thinking of home; of the long lean shadows, of a world stilled by twilight and everything hushed down, of a cuppa on a verandah, an old couple walking the dog and kids called in to tea.

The dark would call me from sleep and I would step into the midnight, I would walk the streets through soft rain dyed orange by the glow of the street lamps. And I felt the city growing over me, clogging me in. And London's air had a texture, a metallic, black lung taste. And I shivered under my shower's thin water after the boiler broke down in my block of flats. And my doona was a skeleton, there was not enough meat in it and I was thinking of you too much. In that first winter, in the ragged time before catching on to sleep, there was a wavering.

And for seventeen years I have stayed.

I wrote in my journal about a savage cliff on the coast that people use to jump off. There was the newspaper article about the man who held onto his lover's coat as she dangled over the edge. 'For God's sake, let me go,' she cried, 'If you don't, then you come with me.' He let go.

There was no word from you on that first birthday away and there's been no word since. Of course not, I didn't give you an address. But I had hoped for some detective work—a phone call to my parents perhaps and some spectacular act, foolish flowers, a rash letter, a doorbell ring.

That first birthday away I wore my black lacy bra, the one just for special occasions. 'The sheepdog bra,' you called it once, 'Because it rounds 'em up and points 'em in the right direction.' I'd laughed and laughed at that. It's recorded in my journal, my rich storeroom of our past. My writing fuel.

Every writer has in them a chip of ice.
Graham Greene

I have trapped my life meticulously.

I took a train into the country in that first winter and my heart lifted as London's vastness thinned and dropped away. I got off at a station by the coast and walked across a field of pebbles that looked like winter snow. I walked to the soft brown, cantankerous, broiling sea and there were furious, spiteful little waves and a nuclear power plant in the distance and as I was pushed and knocked and whipped by the wind I felt for the first time that perhaps, just perhaps, I could be buoyant in all this.

I came home late that night and walked through a fog that was like soft, still rain. A strange exhilaration shot through me, I felt poised, on the brink. I ran my fingers through hair that was still sticky and heavy from ocean-laden wind and I knew that for my spirit to soar, I would have to move on and not back.

And I knew at last what it was I would write.

I have never stayed very long the few times I made the journey back to Australia. It is difficult to face certain people, even after so long. I always meant to ring you and never did; not wanting to confront a put down phone, a refusal to speak, a lawyer's threat. A girlfriend perhaps, a possible wife.

When I was twenty-five I read somewhere that people should rid themselves of their possessions every seven years, or they will start to be owned by them. I arrived in this country with just one suitcase, one painting of my land (bought with the money I had allocated for the wedding dress) and one set of rosary beads—your mother's.

You had folded my fingers over them the last time I saw you. The ends of the crucifix had jabbed into my flesh as I shut my fist tight. And I do not even now have the will to return them, for some part of me still hangs on. And I feel the jab still, in the ragged time some nights when I'm trying to fall into sleep.

I think back with sweet pain, even after so long, of the hurting crispness of the Australian light, of air caressing me like a warm bath, of the sky and the water and the bush that were so insistent in the city I left behind, of the lyricism of words that have vanished from my vocabulary, words like Wollongong, Woolloomooloo, Dubbo, Coonabarabran, Narrabri. And Total Fire Ban and esky, Polly Waffle and ute and perve. Of the looseness of the Australian people, their disarming fresh friendliness, the way they sometimes strike me as so bright and bubbly and insecure, like teenagers growing too tall too fast.

I feel old. A week ago I was walking the city late, on one of my rare forays back into London. The rain came and I did not shy away from it, for the earth softly spattered into my memory, the hint of a smell carried by the wet. I took off my glasses and the world swam and crumbled before me and it was as if the glasses and their sharpness had been holding me together and suddenly I was tumbling within the softness of my flawed vision. I knew in that moment what had to be done, and this story was begun.

The last time I saw you, your hand entwined in mine, was like a handkerchief at my tears. We had sat side by side on a park bench. We did not look at each other. You pleaded with me to reconsider. The church had not yet been cancelled.

With the birth of each child, you lose two novels.
                                                    Candia McWilliam

What have I done? What have I done? For years afterwards I wept.

In the depth of that first English winter I took a train down to my new country home. I stared out the window at the fleeting countryside, so soft and meek and fragile and tamed. Darkness dropped down, and out of the vast blanket of haze that was the sky, a sunset peeped through like a rip in a curtain.

When I stepped from the cab the wind was muscular in the trees. There was fat rain. It was pitch black, so unlike the skyless and starless orange London glow. And deep in that first night the wind buffeted the house I had chosen, this lopsided old cottage that I still use as my base near the nuclear power plant by the sea. The rain spattered in gusts like rice flung at intervals onto a window, then the thunder came and the house murmured with it. The channel was restless and wild nearby and the sound of the water agitated; it didn't soothe, it teased and taunted the gypsy in me and the choices I had made.

On that first morning in this house I woke at seven twenty five. It was still dark, it was as if the day and the light had slept in. At seven forty five there was pink in the sky but the day was so reluctantly dragged from the night. Then as the winter light came stealing in I sat on the windowseat and the beautiful sun repaired me. I felt a great sadness and loneliness wash over me and it was vivid and glittering and searing. I picked up my notepad. I wrote. I felt a strange exhilaration lifting me high. I mined my journals. My name is Disturbance. The betrayal had begun.

> *Exile is not a word*
> *It is hands joined in*
>   *supplication*
> *In an empty cathedral*
>
> Peter Woods

RAIMONDO CORTESE

Theatre as Organic Disorder

It is not uncommon for people who work in the theatre to be asked: why do it? Working in film or television would appear to be a legitimate occupation, but theatre? If you say, in my case, that writing for theatre is your preference, it is assumed, although you won't admit it, that your work simply isn't good enough for the big screen. Perhaps you have been unjustly neglected and are waiting to be discovered by a producer. At best, you are met with disbelief. Working in the theatre, we are told, is a struggle. So much time and energy invested and for what? Nobody goes anymore and, let's face it, the money is shit. Yet those who have worked in the theatre persist throughout their lives in returning to it. Actors and directors have been known to knock back lucrative work in television for the pleasure of being in a co-op share production, seen by a handful of their friends. The belief is held that theatre is a return to the 'craft', a welcome respite from the world of professional entertainment fodder. Their friends tell them that they loved the show, but they must be mad. They probably are, for what happens in the theatre is close to madness.

Does this imply that theatre is undergoing a crisis, as is so often suggested? Of course not. Theatre continues to be done because people love doing it, with or without financial support. Its importance has been defined in terms of a synthesis of all arts forms, but what makes theatre essential to the way we live is, above all else, because it is 'live'. That is why it is such a powerful means of expression. No matter how harsh the historical attempts to suppress it, it continues to survive. Our lives might be assailed by technologies that separate us from a sense of community, but our desire for theatre, in all its infinite forms, is invulnerable. The crisis is not within theatre, but within the tired conventions that generally surround professional theatre culture. The problem is the way we do it.

Over the years, much of what we call professional Australian theatre has been watered down to an ineffectual parody in order to re-affirm the dreary values of its tiny middle-class WASP audience. At best they might seek the odd pinch on the arse as a naughty diversion. Most simply want to be empowered to acknowledge each other and say, 'Look at me, I've turned up tonight, therefore I must be cultured. And while you're at it, you might notice what I'm wearing, isn't it marvellous!' This is, of course, a far cry from a theatre culture that arises from its own essential need to be 'live'. In fact, whatever qualities that are deemed 'live' and therefore theatrical are consciously removed. What we end up with is an institutionalised culture at its most degenerate; a dead convention of theatre so feeble that it can't stand up without the full scale support of production values. The actors are not required to inhabit their work, but rather to demonstrate what they've learnt by rote. They are told: 'Don't worry if nothing is happening, there will be plenty of music and lovely costumes so the audience won't notice.' Is it any wonder that the vast majority of the public regard this stuff as boring crap.

Theatre, with its traditions that go back thousands of years, does not seek such trite outcomes. It was designed to hit us in the guts. Our sense of the real, everything we assume to be true about ourselves, should be shattered, or as Kafka nicely expressed it, it is 'an axe to the frozen sea within us'. Theatre is a social exorcism, not on any literal level, but through a mysterious association of forces. The mythical realm collides with our conscious minds while we, as the audience, are in the very act of being witness.

Theatre owes its origins to the primitive rite. In the diverse rituals that persist today in tribal societies, the bodies of the participants are usually inflicted with markings or wounds. Sometimes flesh is torn, or pegs are inserted through limbs, chest and face, or the skin is engraved with razor sharp tools, then rubbed with coloured ashes. The experience can be so painful, that the initiate often collapses into unconsciousness several times before the ordeal is over. When the rite of passage is completed, the physical scarification is all that remains. The language of theatre is thus encoded on the body, lodged in the memory and social awareness of the initiate so profoundly that it shapes the rest of their lives. It is a way of keeping the disparate nature of human beings together.

In Greek drama, characters are axed in the bath, engulfed by fiery garments, boiled in vats of blood, have their eyes ripped out or fall victim to flesh-eating plagues. Babies are stabbed and cooked up for their parents in sumptuous style. Sons fuck their mothers, daughters their fathers. Patricide, matricide, fratricide and general tyranny are common. The Romans, that race of soldiers and engineers apt to take things literally, preferred to do away with pretence and perform their slaughters for real. The Colosseum and provincial amphitheatres became the ideal venues for pitched battles decorated with corpses. Tortures were practised on religious heretics and political opponents of the regime, with a degree of inventiveness encouraged by the officials—all before thousands of cheering fans, who apparently shared a proclivity for human ingurgitation by lions or bears. The plays of Shakespeare and the Jacobeans, while offering a welcome return to theatre's metaphysical potential, are nonetheless riddled with incest, murder, scatological references, sex and an infinite array of human skullduggery. I suspect that most of our theatre critics would be horrified to experience the power of a genuine production of Shakespeare. Nor would the carnal and gastronomic obsessions of the Commedia dell'Arte go down any better. The great theatre of the twentieth century has continued this tradition of theatre as social exorcism; from Strindberg through to the German expressionists, Artaud's Theatre of Cruelty, Horvath, Beckett, or the dark psychological world of Pinter, or Fassbinder, or the dreamscapes of Robert Wilson and Heiner Muller, or the work by such contemporary companies as The Wooster Group, The Mali Theatre of St Petersburg, De La Guarda and Societas Raffaello Sanzio to name but a few. All see theatre as something living and tangible.

For Plato the ritual was a necessary means for 'correcting those circuits of the head that were deranged by learning to know the harmonies of the world'. This is the opposite of conventional psychiatry which encourages patients to rationalise their unconscious drives. Rather, mental healing occurs simply through the experience of being present to the rite.

Intelligence and the realm of functional reality are left light years behind. The soul is briefly unified with the mind, or according to Artaud: 'actions are made to coincide with thoughts'. It is implied here that consciousness, or what we learn to accept as normal, can inhibit us, so that we constantly check ourselves before committing to action. This, of course, is Hamlet's classic dilemma—he rationalises instead of doing what he knows he must do—kill that motherfucker Claudius. The audience are one step ahead of him. They can already glimpse the consequences of his failure to act (most of them already know the play). The court around the unhappy prince slowly crumbles through treachery while clowns render up their perverse re-inactments. By the time thought and action coalesce at the end of the play, it is too late. This is classic tragedy. 'Your character is your fate' as Chekhov wrote (or words to that effect). Nobody can avoid it, for fate is simply the external manifestation of our true selves. Avoidance or self-denial will only promote a tragic outcome. Had *Hamlet* been a comedy, then the Dane might have acted first, thought later, in a manner that showed no regard for consequences. He might well have slain Claudius and fucked Ophelia in the first act with an attitude of 'who cares, let come what may'.

Western society, like its historical predecessors, is obsessed with cruelty and pornography. It sells. The media could never make a profit without indulging us with lurid details. That was figured out by the London editor of the *Times* hundreds of years ago when he outstripped his rivals by reporting on the murder victims floating in the Thames. Sex, in particular, is used to sell a plethora of junk. Newspapers are fixated daily on the horrors of war, natural disasters and the sexual misdemeanours of the rich and powerful. They claim to be keeping us informed. But it serves a deeper, less quantifiable purpose. We need it. The media is merely fulfilling what the theatre has always done. The rich and famous must appear fallible, so that we can be like them. We might raise them to great heights but we demand our revenge at every opportunity. That is our democracy, a commodified manifestation of our unconscious violence. The more imploded and sanitised our existence becomes, the more likely we will rely on the media to dredge up whatever desperate, recycled forms of horror and pornography it can find. Our shadow is expunged through an excess of entertainment cruelty, in the belief that it never affects us directly. It thrills us. We become obsessed though we never see the results. We are not permitted to experience the direct consequences of the carnage. The information is random and exotic, difficult to feel a part of. The trash media ultimately does little to shake our souls. All we experience are the cravings of a junkie for the next daily dose. The death of Princess Diana was perhaps an exception. People had followed her story for years, day in, day out. After her death, psychiatric appointments in the United Kingdom reputedly dropped by two thirds—the populace healed through national mourning. Her public funeral is an example of mass theatre. We need tragedy to maintain our sanity.

Theatre takes us from go to woe. From the first seeds of despair, as in *King Lear*, *The Seagull*, and *Death of a Salesman*, through to the final moment of grief shared with the audience—the mass that concludes with the eating of the transubstantiated body and blood of Christ. The health of a society can be measured by the quality and quantity of dramatic *tragedy* it produces. The Golden Age of Greece and Elizabethan England were both prosperous and sophisticated times from which emerged embryonic democracies. Both were also periods where *tragedies* flourished. Comedy, especially of the satirical variety, is more likely to arise from cynical or tyrannical periods in history, such as in the heyday of the Commédia del'Arte in Italy around the time of Machiavelli, or the Comedie Française during Moliere's day, or during the Great Depression of the 1930's where only musical comedies seemed to prosper (and also their nostalgic revival in the nineties). A healthy society is one that is not afraid to face its demons. By doing so, it ensures that our unconscious needs are ritualised instead of distorted into a means of repression.

Kafka's story *In the Penal Colony* captures perfectly the most fundamental problem facing much of what we call theatre in this country. The story not only deals with the birth of language but also how the implosion of our creative energies into conscious and reductive mechanisms can only serve to destroy us. It is a modern day scarification ritual that precedes the horrors of Hitler's extermination camps. Kafka has chosen to invert the violence, for the weight of the past is already upon us (consciousness checks us before we commit ourselves to action). We are born condemned 'to a continuum of disease', as William Gaddis put it, though unaware of the crime we have committed. Thus the officer in the penal colony volunteers for his own torture. He straps himself into the machine, whose needles bear down on him and tattoo his unnamed crime into his skin. The machine, quite typically, is faulty and begins to self-destruct. The inscription turns into sheer murder. The man is stabbed to death by thousands of skewers until body and mechanical parts become indistinguishable. The face of the corpse is as calm and unknowing as it was in life. Unlike the ecstasy of the tribal initiate or the rapture on the face of Bernini's St Therese, there is no sign of deliverance.

Most theatre in Australia today is tame. The emphasis is clearly on wet social satire. The notion of Australian *tragic* drama is almost non-existent. Our theatre seeks to comfort rather than provoke. It tells its audience, 'Yes, whatever you think about yourselves is right.' It's saturated by a self-conscious and literal view of political and poetic experience. Perhaps we as an audience are unwilling to acknowledge the tragic dimensions of our historical past, not only with the treatment of Aborigines, but also our violent convict heritage and the mindless terror that led much of our immigrant population to flee to the 'lucky country', not to mention the ongoing displacement felt by the second generation. The *tragedy* of this turbulent and brutal history pervades our contemporary psyches. Theatre cannot afford to neglect its role of forging our essential mythology from this everyday reality.

Professional theatre in Australia is largely caught between two schools of practice, neither of which owe their allegiance to ritual. The first was born out of nineteenth century melodrama—a particularly dull school of theatre that was institutionalised by rich ninnies like Stanislavsky (whose ridiculous precepts are unfortunately taught in the majority of our acting schools). In essence it aims toward a 'presentation' or 'staging' of the play. It is a kind of theatre that thrives from an external convention of what theatre is or should look like. It is a convention defined by a brief rehearsal period that does not allow enough time for the actor to inhabit the 'play'. The actor's work ends up being a demonstration, barely responsive to being 'live', or in other words, to what is actually happening on stage, as the action unfolds. Instead, the emotional life of the play is already gridded which means that the actor is required to go into replay night after night—they must pretend to feel. This spurious feat is achieved through a technical approach to the work. It becomes a matter of the right delivery. This theatre's reliance, therefore, is on stagecraft, which, rather than show the actor as a living organism, seeks to mask what is really happening. The potential for real theatre to occur is nullified. In fact, the bigger the lie, the more successful is deemed the production. This convention has been so pervasive in Australia that the majority of our plays are churned out to complement it. They are plays that revel in the discussion of external ideas, but have little internal action. The written text becomes a bible, without room for collaboration or interpretation. The actors become no more than mouthpieces for a particular viewpoint. In an attempt to offset the tedious nature of this drivel, the playwrights try to commit themselves to interesting topics, while the directors emphasise nice 'shaping' or blocking (with some much needed help from the designer) and the actors do their best to perform their guts out, replete with large gestures and plenty of hollow emotion. Plays that have inherent dramatic action are usually neglected by the major companies because they are not 'about' anything. Very often artistic directors are unable to see much beyond the limitations of the existing convention, nor are they capable of developing acting methods that aim towards anything more than an external 'presentation'. Those few audiences that appreciate this sort of crap, together with the theatre critics who have grown up with it, determine the quality of all other theatre against it.

The other dominant school of theatre in Australia is that of a younger, middle-class, so-called rebellious breed that has emerged largely out of universities. Its main thrust is that theatre should reject narrative (a view of narrative that is extremely narrow) and instead be generated by a physical manifestation of 'ideas'. Why is this bastard child just as trite as its parent? Because it cannot deal with the fundamental, dynamic relationship between actors or performers on stage and their relationship to their audience. Anyone who seeks to control or override the living, dramatic moment, what Artaud calls 'the frail moving force', between actors, with external values (so often born out of coffee table theory) fails to understand the power of theatre. Once again, this type of theatre seeks to impose inane concepts upon the actor that are often frighteningly literal. Sometimes bold design ideas are thrown in, or bold performance styles are appropriated, but the acting, the 'work', is again demonstrative and denied its growth within a dynamic evolution. And yet if we refuse to enjoy this trivial entertainment we are told that it is because we don't understand it. The emphasis here, even more so than its conservative drawing-room forebears, is on heavy-handed production values that mask the fact that nothing is happening between the actors.

The energised presence of the actor, the clown, or the Kathakali dancer with an oil lamp is far more captivating than video screens and other forms of design-driven distraction because they are genuinely 'live', not just trotting through the motions with bleary eyes because a director, who has read too much Derrida for their own good, has instructed them to. These directors, as with their parents, do not have the ability to facilitate a dynamic acting process that allows the 'work' to live and breathe in a theatrical environment. They are, in fact, charlatans, merely trying to cover their own tracks by keeping the stage busy with physical activity. A product of the cultural cringe, they like to be informed about theatre, but have no instinct for it. The majority of the public are even further alienated, though their productions are attractive to a tiny, pretentious, pseudo-intelligentsia, a more fad form of the subscriber elite, who wish to be told they are clever and are disparaging towards emotional engagement. I shall again quote a line from Artaud, which is particularly pertinent to much of this superficial nonsense: 'And if there is one truly infernal thing left today, it is our artistic dallying with forms, instead of being like those tortured at the stake, signalling through the flames'. What Artaud craves, as do all serious theatre makers, is to glimpse the essential living spirit that drives us as human beings. Theatre provides the nexus for the actor to drop their mask. The audience witness humanity beneath all the apparel of social conformity. It is refreshing to see that a number of small self-funded theatre companies have emerged in recent years, particularly in Melbourne, Sydney and Adelaide, which are returning to the basics of the acting craft.

What engages us in theatre, I believe, is something inexplicable—a sense of awe, similar to the rush or fall from being awoken from a dream, symbolised by the hashish eating assassins in the court of Hasan-i Sabbah diving off their mountain fortress of Alamut (meaning 'eagle's nest') to their deaths in the valley below. The unconscious pours freely through us when we experience ritual. Thought and action are entwined. Suddenly we behold what is 'real', the organic disorder that fills our every action. The 'real' is experience in its totality, the shadow forever stalking what we express through the words we have at our disposal. The 'real' is the surge of energy that Plato calls our soul harmonising with our minds. The artist of the theatre must dive into this gulf that separates us from total experience, between our hyper-rational, functional existence and the mysterious, the un-nameable. The theatre must aim to release us to the ecstasy of our imaginative and emotional limits.

This happens not only in theatre, but also when we read or watch sport. We glimpse it in life all the time, providing we are open to seeing it, providing we have allowed our perceptions to be tilted. Theatre wants us to regain our most basic childhood perception, to look at everything anew, rather than with the stale inert indifference we glance about the world that is known to us, that we have lost the ability to reinvent. All babies are born synaesthetic. When we touch a baby's hand we awaken a total sensory experience. The baby will experience stimulation from all five senses, as it will if you dangle keys in front it—apart from hearing an array of sounds, the baby will experience taste, colours will shoot into its visual field, tactile sensations will tremor through its body, odours will fill its tiny nostrils. No wonder so many of the enlightenment poets experimented with opium and mushrooms that produce a similar synaesthetic response (not to mention LSD). Messian, Nabakov and Kandinsky didn't have to indulge in drugs as they, like a fraction of the adult population, retained a degree of natural synaesthesia throughout their lives.

So how do we create this total theatre, a theatre that seeks to take us beyond the boundaries of self-imposed exile? I do not believe it is difficult. Certainly we must throw out the conventional theatre as it is practised. But it is not necessary to concern ourselves with the tired and pedantic debate over forms. Any theatre can be 'alive'. It is not a question of form, it is a question of 'presence'. When Nietzsche declared God dead he unwittingly unleashed a hyper-rational contagion that swept through the arts of the twentieth century. The obsession with the word as subject, or the form as subject, has thankfully run out of steam long ago. This academic preoccupation undermines the pleasure of experiencing art for what it is. Our appreciation becomes self-conscious. The theatre can forget about forms. All forms can attain theatre. This is not to say ideas are not important, but forms and ideas should be imbedded within the work and not exist externally to it, as in so much puerile theatre where actors are used to express ideas literally, either verbally or with visual choreography. And although directors and writers of these works genuinely believe they are smart, the aim of theatre should never be to convince us that we have something to learn. We should undergo an exorcism. Nor do we require Artaud's nostalgic neo-primitivism. Often the most simple dramatic situations can achieve it, for it is apparent in everyday life. But in theatre we get to share it as ordained participants. Instead of concerning ourselves with the pathetic attempts at dazzling our audiences with technological wizardry, which some arts bureaucrats seem to think is the way of the future, we should focus once more on the art of the actor. It is the 'live' actor that makes theatre what it is. They are the centre of gravity. If we can't get that right, then no amount of ornamentation will make the theatre work.

The work must happen on the floor during rehearsal, a kind of work that responds to the immediacy of being fully aware. From moment to moment, the actor should not know what will happen next. If they do, it looks self-conscious and artificial. The actor can never lie. They too easily betray themselves. The audience can see a lie from a mile away. The dramatic moment should unfold as it happens. Each time the emotional stakes are played for real, which ensures that the relationship between the actors and the audience is dynamic. The actor is connected to a truthful, fully realised emotion. If they remain connected to each other in a way that is simple, immediate, totally focused, the energy between them and their world will captivate the audience and will always be exciting.

This is the opposite to much of what we see in Australian theatre where the emphasis is on a technical proficiency that masks the emotional life of the character. But the theatrical experience cannot exist without this dynamic, emotionally charged continuum. The world that is created each night before the audience is 'live' and can never be repeated. The actor should always be in the present, focused on what is happening as it happens. As soon as the actor thinks, or wonders if they can manufacture something, then the moment is lost. It only takes a split second for this to be apparent. The audience will be lost and once they're lost, it is very difficult to draw them back again. Of course the words are learnt, perhaps many of the moves may be more or less determined, but these are vacuums. What is really happening on stage is the invisible ripples between the actors, a situation where 'fuck off' can be a vote of confidence, or a rebuff, or an invitation to have sex. Words themselves do not define what happens on stage, they simply offer a guide, a good guide, but that is all. The line 'you make me puke' can be said a thousand times and mean a thousand different things, depending on a range of circumstances that have led up to that particular utterance. Meaning on stage is defined by the actor's choice of action. The choice of action reveals the enormous gulf between our inner drives and our conscious needs. Everything in between is who we are. That is unquantifiable. That is why true theatre is always a surprise. The audience only want to see actors exercise their total free will. It is this free-floating desire or free will that enables the actor to engage in a continuous act of creation, to be present to it. It gives them the strength to embrace action. Theatre is the enemy of the literalists who want to turn our stages and our lives into a banal and ordered reading, where everything is about stating surface content. The internal instruments are beyond our control and it is these that theatre aims to reveal to their full potential. This is what gives life to our existence and what ritual strives to release. This is what is happening when we see theatre that is truly 'live'.

But from day one, what passes for much of theatre culture demands that the actor should lie. When actors audition, they are required to have learnt their lines so they can perform them on stage alongside someone they have probably only just met. And yet if theatre is about the dynamic between them, how can this relationship be conjured truthfully in a few minutes of an audition? It can't. An honest actor would simply do a line reading and probably not get the job. The actor is actually being asked to fake it, to perform their tits off, to lie. To do all the things that make theatre terrible. The actor who lies best generally gets the job. For that is the convention of theatre. Pretend as much as you like, just pretend well. And of course those subscribers to our theatres, who go because it is a social occasion and have been doing so for fifty years, together with the critics who have come to accept that theatre is not 'real' but an artifice, they will regard this lifeless theatrical lie as the penultimate achievement on stage. It's good hamming, that's all it is. Good bullshit. And because the stakes aren't real, nothing happens and the audience walk away having invested nothing and experienced nothing. There are, and have been, many notable exceptions to this fallacy in Australian theatre—including work produced by La Mama, The Pram Factory, Nimrod, Anthill, The Church and various independent companies, as well as the work of a number of artists that have pursued their love for theatre in the last few years despite meagre funding levels. But much of what we see is the result of prolonged stagnation, so it is no surprise that audiences, especially those under thirty, are hard to find. The simple truth is, they don't believe what they see. Who can blame them? Who wants to see theatre that demonstrates either the moribund skills of traffic control or the vacuous titillation of dilettantes who seek to flatter us with literality and whose actors strut about with puffed up feathers?

A director who knows what acting is would simply use an audition process to discover how well the actor works on the floor, their ability to focus and connect with the other actors. But they would not demand an on the spot performance rendered from work done in isolation. The rehearsal should then set up various processes that allow the actor to be vulnerable to the possibilities of change, so that they are open and willing, are 'alive'. The actor must therefore shed their attitudes towards acting. Technique generally masks what is, rather than acts as a conduit for what is. There is always something happening and the task of the director is not to block it, but to help it flow unimpeded. Technique is better stripped away. I prefer to see an actor that is technically incompetent but alive to what is happening than all that professional stagecraft that is so caught up in itself, a bomb could explode with no effect on the performance. The actor is not a vehicle for the text, but nor is the performance a vehicle for the actor to show off their skills. It is boring. The writer, the director and actor, and the production artists, should aim towards invisibility. Only the charlatans love to pop their heads up so as to be noticed, which is profoundly annoying and provokes our desire to behead them.

The rehearsal period does not need to aim towards an arrival of the 'work', it is a process of unlearning that casts off the notion that an actor or a character should behave in any particular way. There is no such thing as a scripted character anyway. The writer only creates a semblance of a character which is inhabited by the actor and is ninety percent them. To be 'in character' does not mean that we should constrict the parameters of what we think is believable. Everybody behaves unpredictably all the time. When in life are we limited by the notion that we can't do such and such because it would be 'out of character'? We simply do what we do as the circumstances hit us. Everybody behaves with this disregard for 'character', yet everybody makes wild assumptions about other people's 'character'. The theatre is a place where these restrictions are irrelevant. What a character does depends on the dramatic moment and proceeds from there. Too often we confuse naturalism or natural acting with normalism. This is an attempt to place controls on the actor's spirit. It is not what creates good acting. The actor simply needs to put their focus on the person they are talking to or on what is actually happening between them. What is happening will shape what that actor does and that will make the audience believe the actor is a character.

The play or production is ready to be performed when the actors are no longer in control of what will occur, for only then is the situation dynamic and theatrical. If we seek to place constraints on the way the actor feels at any given moment, then the theatre loses its edge and becomes dead. Theatre thrives on emotional energy: without it, it cannot exist. But emotional energy cannot be fixed. You cannot find an emotion during rehearsal and then try to duplicate that moment on stage, as though by practising today will make you do it better tomorrow. The duplication will always be a poor second. It also reveals the actor 'working', which is hideous to watch. Each time will be different and no actor should concern themselves with what they found on the previous night. Directors who tell the actor to remember their emotional peaks and valleys do not understand theatre. Yet we see it all the time—actors pretending to get angry, pretending to cry (with hands conveniently placed over the face in an attempt to shield the facade), pretending to care. Emotional reality is what is happening as it happens. If the actor doesn't feel like crying then they shouldn't. Forget what the writer or the director says, dictating emotions isn't their job. Pretending just kills the moment stone dead. Thanks to melodrama the theatre is full of such bullshit. When a moment is faked the audience will only doubt everything that led up to that point and beyond it.

Within everyday life, most of us are locked into a narrow perception of what we term experience. At least, we exist within a definition of reality that closes off possibilities that are alien to us. We have rationalised away mystery and spirituality from our daily existence. Whether or not one accepts or believes in the multidimensional, dynamic nature of the universe, we do accept that no two human beings are the same. People experience the same phenomena in vastly different ways. It is my belief that theatre is a ritualisation of worldly happenings, allowing us to transcend our functional existence, so that we share an initiation as a community. It disorders our sense of the 'real', releasing us from the confines of the conscious world. The theatre is a ritual of transitions, from one moment to another, in a continuous process. Sometimes the transition is momentous and painful, at other times it is barely noticed, if at all, or if we do become aware of it, it is too late and has already transformed into something else, or has swept us along in a huge current that we have no real understanding of and certainly no words to describe. This is the theatre that reminds us that we are not alone, that we are part of something far beyond ourselves. It reveals the magical dimension of ourselves in the most subtle ways, among simple conversations between strangers, a cry of joy, a surprise, obscure gestures and movements that we might use in greeting, in the way we avert our eyes in embarrassment, or laugh at something we recognise, that perhaps makes us uncomfortable. It is the accumulation of these subtle details that makes us human, that enables us to experience the most profound feelings without ever really knowing why. This is not the realm of the conscious mind, or ideas, or the egoism of the spectacle. It is the world we ignore, or assume does not exist, that is not worthy of institutionalised theatre culture, of television cameras or newspapers or history books. It is the un-nameable, call it soul if you like, that reveals its true character in every second of every minute if only we were aware of it. Only in the ritual of the 'live' event (and theatre is only one such event) do we as an audience get to play the part of silent angels, to participate and experience these subtleties and by doing so, share our initiation as a community of people from a comfortable state into one of super-awareness. Afterwards, of course, all might be forgotten.

ROBERT DESSAIX

A Mad Affair

Jack! Is that you? Beryl peered across the lawn strewn with cockatoos at the sauntering figure in the red checked shirt, ambling down the path towards the gate. She'd have called out, but something clutched sharply at her throat. Jack ambled on. Those sinewy legs, that lazy grace. Oleanders, Jack, oleanders, Jack. And then he vanished.

Typical, Beryl said quite sharply to nobody. It was typical of Jack to taunt her like that. Amazingly warmed by the clear sun, Beryl sat on her bench and gazed across the lawn at the other patients, alone and in clutches, wandering the paths, dozing in plastic chairs or just standing stock-still and hunched in their faded dressing-gowns, like dead rose bushes.

Suddenly the lunch bell went. Tinkle, tinkle, tinkle. *Blinkle, hinkle, finkle*, said Beryl, not crossly, but with a tetchy edge she was known for. She sat and watched the tide turn in the garden, the dressing-gowns and wheelchairs first dithering and then drifting slowly back towards the house, like strands of seaweed. The cockatoos pecked on, a brilliant white against the green.

Bugger lunch, said Beryl with a certain resonance. Actually, her voice had always been one of her good points (although obviously not good enough). Teachers had remarked on it. She had even once taken up French. *Voulez-vous danser avec moi?* she said, as the tinkling started up again (shriller this time). Beautiful word, '*danser*'. Beryl watched Tommy Smith stagger into a wheelbarrow and fall over. *Voulez-vous danser avec moi?* she said again, silkily, smiling to herself. Such pleasure to the tongue.

Jack had had a beautiful voice as well. Rich and throaty. Especially in the bus—sorry, *coach*—that first time. How she blushed when he said: 'What do you mean, "Is it time to get back on the bus?" What's this "bus" business? It's a coach, Miss Mackie, it's time to get back on the coach.' And grinned. 'Am I then your princess?' she thought, taking his warm, firm, gallant hand lightly and stepping up into the bus, hardly heaving at all. Beryl had never been slight. 'Who looks twice at a girl who's all skin and bones?' her mother had said. 'No man wants a skinny little stick of a thing.' Her mother had been wrong about this, and much else besides.

Goodness knows why she went on that tour. No, actually, that wasn't right—she knew perfectly well why. She was lonely. Desperate, her friend Lily said, who wouldn't have been caught dead (so she said) taking a coach tour anywhere. A plain girl, Lily, plain as a mud fence, to be perfectly honest, no figure to speak of and an unfortunate mouth, but she had a way with her. When it came to boys, as it did with Lily, she just had a way with her. It was a mystery to Beryl. She didn't seem to have a way with her at all.

When she first left school (Tommy Smith was still flailing on the ground, Nurse McIntyre swooping like a fat blue beetle) and started working in the office at the knitting factory, it didn't seem to matter. Or not much. No one minded if she joined them for lunch in the canteen, one or two of the men even flirted with her occasionally … well, they didn't exactly flirt, but at least made teasing remarks and laughed. And were gone. 'The thing is, Beryl, people really respect you,' one of the girls had said—she remembered it as plain as day: the sodden handkerchief in her hand, the washroom echoes, and the beautiful, empty, weekend face in the mirror, lips pouted, lipstick gleaming in one hand. Beryl laughed now, *laughed right out loud*, pinning Tommy Smith to the path with her eyes as Nurse McIntyre galloped off for a wheelchair—well, you had to laugh. RESPECT? WHO IN GOD'S NAME WANTS RESPECT? *Desired*, Beryl said to Tommy Smith, miles away beyond the cockies, *I wanted to be desired. I didn't even respect myself. Who gives a fucking rat's arse whether Gordon Dunlop from Despatch respected me or not?*

Beryl never said 'fucking'—not ever ever. Nor 'arse'. It was just that she'd heard Clive the handyman telling someone or other behind the rhododendrons that he didn't give a fucking rat's arse whether Saturday was convenient or not, and the phrase had struck her as radiantly beautiful. It had gone into her left ear, down some canal or other and got stuck at the base of her tongue. Then one morning when Nurse McIntyre had asked her in that jolly, wheezy voice of hers if she'd like to sit in the sun for a while, she'd said: 'I don't give a fucking rat's arse either way.' The effect had been dazzling and multicoloured. It was odd the way some words just got stuck to your tongue and couldn't be spat off. 'Bishop Tutu', for example. Beryl spat, opened her mouth and heard *Bishop Tutu* come out again. Yes, it was still there.

There must have been a couple of dozen other passengers on the tour. Couples mostly, a retired schooteacher or two, a lady from Birmingham with her sister, a rather stand-offish young librarian—hard to remember now. And like a beacon of light at the front of the bus sat Jack in his red checked shirt and shorts. Jack drove and joked and handed people on and off the bus. Half the time Beryl found she wasn't taking in the mountains or the Murray or even Canberra because her eyes were on the deeply tanned nape of Jack's neck between the ducktails and the red checked collar, and her ears were living a life of their own, deep inside his dark, warm voice, which made her think of smoothly shaved skin and being kissed. And on the last night, in a hotel dining-room smelling of schnitzel and floor polish, he asked her to dance, and she touched his shoulder blades, which were sharp and angelic all at once, and he looked at her with a look. *Yes, a look*, Beryl said, watching Tommy Smith begin to jerk oddly on the grass beside the barrow. *He saw into me and I saw into him.* And that instant, that minuscule moment of being … *beholden* (said Beryl, still partly Presbyterian) swelled to fill the whole world. Even the sky that night was cramped by comparison.

Back home in Melbourne Beryl was not herself at all. 'What's wrong with you, Beryl?' her mother said, eyeing her oddly. 'You're not yourself at all.' Beryl laughed too loudly, voiced strong opinions and secretly took up cigarettes. The wooziness, the burning, the unslaked craving—and the ashes at the end—it was hard to remember now what was Jack and what was Ardath. She roared the hymns of a Sunday morning. And wept in the darkness at the pictures with her sisters. And a week or two later sent Jack a card at the depot inviting him home to lunch.

Her mother, pleasantly alarmed, made a steak and kidney pie. Jack flirted with Beryl's sisters in a breezy sort of way, told tales of tours gone wrong and talked buses and trucks with Beryl's father, who sat bolt upright at the end of the table as if acting the part of an embarrassed man in a badly written play. (Nurse McIntyre was pelting down the path now towards the spasming stick figure on the grass, with Malcolm the paramedic joggling a wheelchair along behind her. There was a faint clinking sound and the whiff of brussels sprouts drifting across from the dining-room.)

Everyone was charmed by Jack and when he'd sauntered off down to the tram-stop alone ('Please don't bother—I'll be fine') they all agreed it had gone well. But Beryl felt she'd hardly been there. She took off the lilac dress she'd bought the day before and hid it at the back of the wardrobe.

Jack never came again. Beryl could hardly breathe. She waited two weeks and took a weekend tour to Ballarat, but the driver was a large, fair-haired man with a 'better half' and four 'nippers' at home in Prahran. Unravelling and pulling apart, Beryl then went to Adelaide, but the driver was a cheery Englishman who hadn't even heard of Jack. Beryl went to Bendigo on a Gold Fields Tour, to the Snowy Mountains, to Gippsland and Lakes Entrance, she went on a City Lights tour late one Friday night, she even went up the Murray again and on to Canberra. But no Jack. The exploding moment shrank to a pinprick and Beryl's soul crumpled. *A pinprick*, Beryl whispered, as they lifted Tommy Smith, suddenly limp, into the wheelchair.

Yet, strange to relate, the more Jack disappeared, the more Beryl seemed to see him. It was as if she'd hit upon some undiscovered principle. Soon after the trip to Ballarat she saw him jump down out of a delivery van at the knitting factory. The strong, brown legs, the wavy hair, the ambling walk around to the far side of the truck ... but when he re-emerged he was curiously no longer Jack, just a nondescript delivery man, just a man, not Jack at all. Beryl felt tricked. And then she'd see him in a queue at the butcher's or several rows away at the pictures or through a train window or up a ladder mending a roof. (Nurse McIntyre suddenly looked up and nailed Beryl to her bench. A moment later she and Malcolm were clattering up the path at speed towards the infirmary, Tommy just a lolling bundle in the chair. Beryl had a sudden memory of his papery skin.)

Even here, where she'd come for a rest all those years ago and never left, she'd seen him once or twice, up to his old tricks. The previous Christmas he'd been dressed up as Father Christmas and when he'd touched her elbow (she knew that touch) and said: 'Enjoying your dinner, darling?' she'd picked up her plum pudding and hot custard and smashed it into his face. It was just too cruel, it was insufferable. A bit of trouble over that.

Beryl stared at the ragged cockies. Funny little clown-like faces. It wasn't that her life had been meaningless exactly, there'd been plenty of meaning if you looked for it, things had happened and had had meaning. And there was God looking at her all the time, which gave things meaning, even watching the cricket on television, although the previous Thursday (Australia vs Pakistan) it had dawned on her that God had given far too little sign of His presence, despite countless opportunities. In fact, none that she could remember. But no, it wasn't meaning that was missing, but something else.

Staring at the black hole of the doorway Tommy Smith had disappeared into was like waiting for a scream. But nothing. Just silence. Beryl considered the cockies, suspecting it was actually one cockie just pretending to be a hundred. Things like that happened sometimes. To tell the truth, sometimes when she glimpsed herself in the mirror, she suspected someone was pretending to be her. But thinking about it made her queasy. No, what was *missing* was any real trace of her ever having been there, that was it. Yet she had been, she had pictures in her head. The horrible thing, the thing that squeezed tears out of her sometimes, was knowing that if she'd never lived her life at all no-one would have noticed. She'd sung her song, but the hall had been quite empty—except for Jack, of course, but he'd only listened to two bars and left.

A big blue beetle was standing in front of her, blocking out the cockatoos. 'Come along, sweetheart, you're missing out on lunch!'

Is that all? said Beryl, and almost chuckled. *Is Tommy Smith dead?*

'Beryl!' said the beetle. 'What a dreadful thing to say! Tommy's just had a little turn. Now come along, let's get you in to lunch.'

Bugger lunch, said Beryl, not moving an inch. She looked up at the beetle and thought, she thinks I'm mad. And then she prayed: Dear God, if you're there, please tell me just one thing—am I mad? The smallest sign would be appreciated.

A voice came: 'Beryl! Come along now, it's steak and kid …'

If you don't mind, said Beryl, *I'm praying.*

One of the cockies poked his head around the beetly blueness and said, eyeing her in the most piercing, yellow fashion: 'The thing is, Beryl, it's not God who isn't there, it's you.'

Beryl shrieked with laughter, dissipating the blueness. *So that's it! What a blessed release!*

Unexpectedly, not being there proved to be a balm. The crumpling and unravelling went away for a start, as did the boiling over with anger, the pressure-cooker feeling she used to get when people did certain things on television, flaunting themselves. Nor did she need to speak much any more, and all those words that had stuck to her tongue like shreds of spinach—'Bishop Tutu' and 'bugger lunch' and one or two old hymns—turned grey and fell apart and she swallowed them. And since she'd become such a 'good girl' now, as Nurse McIntyre (who also wasn't there either, if only she knew it) told her, she was offered Tommy Smith's old room when he failed to come back out of the black hole. A much better room, Tommy's, with a sunny bay-window fit for a cat and a view straight down the path to the main gate. The next time Jack took it into his head to call around, she'd certainly see him coming.

'You're a lucky girl,' Nurse McIntyre trumpeted from the doorway, surveying the very white room with Beryl and her handbag now in it. When all the blueness and waving of arms were gone, Beryl got up from her chair and lowered herself onto the cushioned window-seat to wait.

PAUL COX

My One True Love

For the one true love of my life I want to embrace a rather large picture. The largest of them all. A thing called Death. Please read on …

The first five years of my life during the Second World War, I witnessed nothing but death and destruction. Half the population of the small town we lived in perished.

I was always immensely relieved when I came home and our house was still standing and our neighbours still alive. It caused in me, and others who had crawled from under the ruins, a profound fascination with Death and decay. I kept looking for the skull behind the face. A rather indulgent preoccupation. It wore me out.

But I was extremely fortunate. Found a profession in which I could express myself, learned to treasure life and always tried hard to give both the good and the bad my loving understanding.

Many years later, I met an old man in Nepal with a mission. I met him seemingly by chance—yet I wonder … He was a noble Italian gentleman with a great passion for beauty and the arts. We shared a meal in a small restaurant. A shepherd sang old songs from the old mountains and children offered flowers. It was one of those evenings that help you change.

Before we parted he said, 'When the time comes we must be able to will ourselves to Death.'

He quoted Rilke.

PAUL COX

I would like to walk
out of my heart
under the wide sky.

Then he said, 'Adieu, my friend,' and disappeared into the night. The next morning his body was brought down from the mountain. I saw his face frozen in time and space. A marble sculpture—eyes wide open—his mouth like the Buddha—infinite and timeless—freed from all mortality.

I still see his face. He's always travelled with me and I still carry the little book he gave me. *Tagore's Gitanjali*. In it I read, 'I know I've loved this life and because of that I shall love Death as well.'

I stopped looking for the skull behind the face. Tried to find the human heart. It hasn't been an easy search.

Our civilisation of instant gratification is so out of touch with Death that most people one meets have never seen a dead body. Many die by themselves in white sterile rooms, drugged out of their minds, surrounded by strangers. There's also always some miraculous excuse for Death. Recently I heard that a ninety-seven-year-old man died of cancer. I think he died because he was very old and very tired. May he rest in peace.

We seem to have taken the wrong turn. We don't understand life anymore or love for that matter and consequently are out of tune with Death.

Death, as we know it now, is spending our earnings on things we don't need. Death is the manufacturing of guns, bombs and land mines. Things no-one needs. Death is building cities as drab and grey as possible. Death is emptying the oceans of life and polluting our rivers and waterways. Death is celebrating the wrong gods for the wrong reasons. Death is denying our children to dream of the future. Death is the politics of greed, hatred and ignorance. Death is lost to the living.

My friend from the mountains was right. Poverty and nakedness and even death are nothing, provided we've learned to live without fear.

In the face of Death everything becomes more humane, more alive. In the face of Death only true love makes sense—harmony, peace, warmth, gentleness, kindness, words that have almost disappeared from our vocabulary. All the ambitions, all the career moves become meaningless. In the face of Death we can find our true spirit.

MY ONE TRUE LOVE

All we have to do is return the key and our claims to the house and maybe expect some kind words from families and friends. No more noisy, loud words. People deal in whispers near the dying.

Now we have time for ourselves and can think of all those we have loved and how we have loved them. Life could be like that …

Oh yes, Death is my true love. The true love of my life. I couldn't live without it.

Author Biographies

JOSÉ BORGHINO

José took her in his strong, muscular arms and walked slowly into the lagoon as the light from the full moon flecked the waves around his straining thighs. A gecko barked, a coconut plopped, the moment was lost. Oh dear ...

José Borghino is the Executive Director of the Australian Society of Authors. He lives in Sydney with his lover, Susan, and his two sons, Gabriel and Dominic.

RAIMONDO CORTESE

Raimondo Cortese grew up in Hobart. His mother is an avid reader of European literature and his tenor father sang for thirty years in musicals and opera productions, and so both were encouraging towards Raimondo's nascent theatrical endeavours. He performed in a film and several stage productions as a teenager. At age twenty, he moved to Melbourne and began writing full-time, self-publishing a variety of nonsensical prose which has been confined to a box under his bed. In 1993, a year after his brother Adriano, he graduated from the Victorian College of the Arts School of Drama. They subsequently founded Ranters Theatre Company which premiere all Raimondo's plays, which include *Lucrezia and Cesare, The Fertility of Objects, The Room, Roulette* and *Features of Blown Youth* (which will be touring Europe in 1999). Last year, Text published his collection of short stories, *The Indestructible Corpse* and *The Cat Who Ate Her Master's Soul* is forthcoming.

MIKE COWARD

Journalist, author, cricket commentator and broadcaster Mike Coward will argue over a masala dosa and fresh lime soda, sweet (no ice, please) that true love is most alluring in mid-life. Born in Adelaide in 1946, Coward was 36 before he was beckoned to India. He was deeply affected by this most energising yet enervating of places—one of many seductive contradictions—and, on average, has returned every second year for work or holiday.

Author, editor or ghost writer of six cricket books he was chief cricket writer for *The Advertiser*, Adelaide and *Sydney Morning Herald* and a senior sports writer for the *Age*, Melbourne before opting for the less secure but more fulfilling life as a freelancer. This decision was taken during a two-month sabbatical in the south of India in 1989. Cricket commentator for the *Australian* newspaper since 1992, he can only access a secret file in his electronic diary by entering the name of cricket's peerless contemporary batsman, India's Sachin Tendulkar.

MY ONE TRUE LOVE

PAUL COX
I was born in Holland into a world gone mad, a world at war. After a clumsy, shy childhood, I sailed to Australia in 1963. Following a brief return, I made Melbourne my home. Trained as a photographer, I started a photographic studio and in my spare time, as a hobby, made little movies. I still maintain that if you want to do anything seriously, do it as a hobby. As soon as it becomes a profession, the degree of compromise and mediocrity one has to deal with make it almost impossible to be heard.

I received some recognition in 1981 when I co-wrote and directed *Lonely Hearts*. This was followed by *Man of Flowers, My First Wife, Cactus, Vincent, A Woman's Tale* and many others. Recently I tried to direct *Father Damien* (now *Molokai*), shot in Hawaii with a cast of thousands. Now I'm working on a small film called *Innocence*, and later in the year I will start *Nijinsky*.

My three children are my greatest accomplishment and joy.

PHILIP COX
Philip Cox completed Architecture with honours at Sydney University in 1962 and subsequently was awarded the Royal Australian Institute of Architects' Prize and the NSW Board of Architects Travelling Scholarship.

He has received major awards including the Institute's Gold Medal (1984), Honorary Fellowship of the American Institute of Architects (1987). In 1988 he was awarded the Order of Australia for Services to Architecture. In 1993 he received the inaugural Award for Sport and Architecture from the International Olympic Committee, and in the same year was elected as a fellow of the Royal College of Humanities.

Some of the major works that Philip Cox and his practice, the Cox Group include four major Olympic sports facilities—the Sydney International Aquatic and Athletic Centres, Sydney SuperDome and the RAS Main/Baseball Arena, Sydney Football Stadium, Yulara Tourist Resort at Ayers Rock, Sydney Exhibition Centre and the Australian National Maritime Museum at Darling Harbour.

ROBERT DESSAIX
Robert Dessaix is a broadcaster and now writer living in Melbourne, best known for many years for *Books and Writing*, his weekly literary program on Radio National, as well as the odd review or essay and his translations of Chekhov's plays for the Australian theatre. In recent years he has begun to think of himself more as a writer: in 1994 he published his autobiography *A Mother's Disgrace*, in 1996 his first novel *Night Letters* and in 1998 a collection of stories, essays, talks entitled *(and so forth)*. In between he has edited an anthology of Australian gay and lesbian writing for Oxford University Press and a series of radio interviews with Australian public intellectuals entitled *Speaking Their Minds* (ABC Books). He has few passions apart from language, travel and his friends.

AUTHOR BIOGRAPHIES

GARRY DISHER
When I was asked to write a biographical note that was not of the Garry-Disher-lives-on-the-Mornington-Peninsula-and-is-the-author-of-over-thirty-books variety, but had 'my one true love' in mind, I baulked, for everything in 'Up Above the World' is made up. I'm not very self-reflective by nature, and the exercise smacks of the current Ozlit malaise, concentrating upon the author not the work. But then I saw that one of my minor obsessions had prevailed in 'Up Above the World'—bygone aircraft and seat-of-the-pants flying. It's there in the recent novels, too: crop dusting in *The Sunken Road*, the homicide inspector restoring a Dragon Rapide in *The Dragon Man*, a young man counting the Dornier, Catalina and Empire flying-boats in *Roebuck in The Divine Wind*.

'Up Above the World' is a short story, but it's also notes toward a novel I've been trying to write. Two of my other 'loves' (or interests or obsessions) will help drive it: the effects of war on the lives of ordinary people, and how landscapes are shaped and imagined.

BARRY DIVOLA
Even though Barry Divola made up some of the stuff in *Sissy Bar*, the Dragster bike really existed, and he's still heartbroken that it's no longer in his possession. Last year Barry had his first book published. It was called *Fanclub* (Allen & Unwin). Basically, it was about all the people in front of the stage at pop concerts. Normally Barry writes about all the people on the stage at pop concerts. He has written *Who Weekly*'s music pages since the magazine began in 1992. He has a monthly entertainment column in *Cleo*, reviews movies for *Max*, and also regularly contributes to *Rolling Stone*. If you didn't blink, sneeze or go for a quick piss during the movie *Occasional Coarse Language*, you may have caught his AFI-ignored performance as Derek. He lives with a cat called Uma, and once or (if you're extremely unlucky) twice a year he plays bass in The Fluffy Boys. What do you mean you've never heard of them?

ROBERT DREWE
Robert Drewe was born in Melbourne, grew up in Western Australia and now lives mainly in Sydney. His fiction includes the acclaimed novels *The Drowner, Our Sunshine, Fortune, A Cry in the Jungle Bar* and *The Savage Crows*, and the short story collections *The Bodysurfers* and *The Bay of Contented Men*. His work has been widely translated, won many national and international prizes and been adapted for film, television, radio and the theatre.

DON DUNSTAN
Don Dunstan was a unique, an exotic figure in Australian politics. He was an abundantly gifted politician. As an advocate for reform his achievements were

spectacular. When he dramatically relinquished office in 1979 he left South Australia—particularly Adelaide—deeply changed. For most of a decade he introduced legislation which helped liberalise a State that was seen as among the state's most moribund. Under Don, South Australia was the first state to recognise Aboriginal land rights, pass anti-discrimination laws and introduce a tough code of consumer protection as well as electoral reform.

After Don retired in 1979, he studied and travelled in Italy. In 1994 he indulged his passion for cooking by opening Don's Table, an elegant restaurant in Norwood, featuring many of his own recipes.

Don Dunstan died on 6 February 1999 at the age of 72, after a long battle with cancer.

NIKKI GEMMELL

Nikki Gemmell was born in Wollongong. She moved to Sydney to study writing at the University of Technology and worked as a radio newsreader. She now lives in London with her husband. She is passionate about vaulting skies. Light that bashes me (in England, where I live now, the light licks me). The smell of Alice Springs (how can I cup its fragrance in the palms of my hands, how can I bottle it?). Sleeping in the desert under the stars, being caressed by the air rather than huddling against it. Flinging sun into my lungs. Change. Driving somewhere I've never been, with the ute and the sky and a boxful of tapes. Bush taut with sound. My grandmothers. Grace. Requited love. Mates. Rothko and Rover Thomas. Michael Ondaatje's *Coming Through Slaughter*. God. My handbag collection and my Swiss Army knife and my lovely old drill. Cadbury's Dairy Milk chocolate. My husband.

ELIZABETH JOLLEY

In a reply to the request for an unusual biographical note to accompany my contribution under the title *My One True Love* in this anthology, it would be possible to respond as Judah Waten's mother when Judah, on one occasion, asked her when she was born. (He was curious about her age.)

'I was born, I'm alive as you can see, so what more do you want to know?' she replied so sharply that I never asked her about her age again.

Judah Waten's book, *Alien Son*, gives a first and honest account of a European Jewish family's arrival and settlement in Australia. The author's description of family love and effort parallels my own experience of being much loved in a family of people who would do anything in the world for each other—and for others, as well, when required.

I was born in 1923 and, as you can see, I am still alive. I have a family of three children so it is clear that I have had certain experience among other experiences. I am four times grandmother. My grandchildren are very important to me. When I took my first newly born grandson, Matthew, in my arms I was overwhelmed with love and gratitude for such a gift. I began to understand then, deeply, how much I had been loved and cherished in all sorts of ways by my mother and father and by my grandmother, especially by my grandmother. All this, I had taken for granted ...

NICHOLAS JOSE

I'm a water baby. Scorpio and Dragon. I made the ship journey from London to Adelaide at the age of six months and somehow survived the salmonella I picked up on the rough crossing of the Bight. That was in 1953 and perhaps it was then that I bonded with the sea. We spent our family holidays, from 1965 on, at the beach on South Australia's Yorke Peninsula. There were never many people around and it was easy to love the water in that place, which I have written about in my novel *Paper Nautilus*, published in 1987. My next love was China, which happened when I discovered green tea. Of all the thousands of Chinese characters, it's the ones with the water radical that I like best. Three drops running down the left hand side of the word for 'flow', for example. I worked in China from 1986–1990. Since then I've lived in Harbour City, which I fell in love with back in 1971, when, as a student in Canberra, I made an escape to quench my thirst for the ocean. In that time I've published two novels, *The Rose Crossing* and *The Custodians*. I'm currently working on something inspired by a classic Chinese book called *Six Chapters of a Floating Life*.

ADIB KHAN

Adib Khan was born in Dhaka, Bangladesh where he lived until 1973. That year he came to Australia where he completed a Masters degree in English literature. Khan now lives and works as a teacher in Ballarat.

Seasonal Adjustments was Adib Khan's first novel which won the Christina Stead Prize for fiction and the Book of the Year in 1994 NSW Premier's Prize, was shortlisted for the 1994 Age Book of the Year Award, and won the 1995 Commonwealth Writers' Prize for First Book.

GRETEL KILLEEN

Gretel Killeen is a writer, broadcaster, mother of two and currently non-practising love addict. Her first love affair was at the age of three with her older-man neighbour, three-and-a-half-year-old Hamish. From the age of four, having been dumped for a yo-yo, Gretel spent the next thirteen years seeking affection through inappropriate relationships with animate objects (e.g. boys who went surfing) and inanimate objects (e.g. boys who played football). This was followed by a brief but unattractively expansive love affair with peanut butter and honey sandwiches which lasted until she left high school. Then ensued a series of love affairs with strong silent types (The Dork Period), Italian boys (when they don't speak English they seem so much more interesting), one sailor, one lawyer, one home-handyman (the house needed work) and a mime artist (try having sex with one of them). At the age of twenty-five she fell in love with her newborn son and, at twenty-eight, with her baby daughter. These two love affairs continue. Currently, absolutely desperate for a bloke, she plans to meet, settle down and marry her one true love when she is about sixty-seven.

MEME McDONALD

A love of mine is listening to other people's stories. I was drawn into writing by a group of women, mostly in their seventies, eighties and nineties, who I met at the City Baths in Melbourne. Out of my collaboration with them, we started writing a book. Five years later we had *Put Your Whole Self In* (Penguin) in our arms along with a couple of literary awards.

The Vine grew out of a story told to my partner Boori Pryor. A teacher came up to him after a performance and told of her childhood love for an Aboriginal boy. Where she grew up, a relationship was out of the question, so she nurtured this love in her heart for thirty-six years without telling anyone. This story stayed with me until I could write something to honour it.

With Boori, I have have written two books—*Maybe Tomorrow* (Penguin) and *My Girragundji* (Allen & Unwin)—both ultimately about love and survival. Both of us trying to make up for what we've missed out on in the last 200 years of our country's sorry history. I am very grateful to storytellers, family and writing for keeping love and hope alive in my heart.

DOROTHY PORTER

All my life I have been besieged by infatuations; for transient pretty people as much as transient hobbies, ideas or fads. I have had only one or two truly persistent passions. The most overwhelming of these has been my marriage to reading. It has never left the Honeymoon Suite. My hands still tremble when I first open the fresh pages of a new book. Especially a poetry book. I adore bookshops. I prefer the company of my books to virtually that of anyone except those closest to me—and anyone who can make me laugh. It is a source of amazement to me that I write books myself but writing is more often a frustration than a delight, while reading, no matter where I am or what is happening, remains an unalloyed joy.

MARGARET SCOTT

Most of my life has been spent falling in love with romantic fictions which, time after time, I've tried to impose on unfortunate creatures of flesh and blood. First it was horses who were supposed to act like the wonderfully wise and loyal animals in pony books, then it was young men who were supposed to carry on like Heathcliff. Eventually I met a man who was equally bewitched by the idea of a grand passion, but, like many romantic heroes, he died young. I am fortunate in being left with many people and many things that I love: my children and grandchildren; friends; writing; various poems; novels and plays that I read over and over again; my house and garden and the astonishing, ever-changing land and seascapes of the Tasman Peninsula where I have my home. And I like to think that as I get older I see all these more clearly than I used to see the horses and the Heathcliffs in my youth.

ROSIE SCOTT
Since the age of ten when I wrote my first novel and went on my first anti-apartheid march, life has continued to intrude on my writing on a pretty regular basis. Political activism, a certain obsessive passion for husband and daughters, and numerous other irresistible digressions from my one true love—writing—have however, made for an interesting life, unspoilt by anything as mundane as financial security or any form of future planning in general.

I hope my eighth (and first non-fiction book) *The Red Heart* published this year, will help to explain how my one true love held its own in a lifetime of recklessness.

EMMA TOM
Emma Tom was born in November 1969 and grew up in the unfashionable western suburbs of Sydney followed by the equally unfashionable rural suburban haven of coastal New South Wales.

After a spectacularly fidgety career as a life drawing model, she completed a cadetship on a rural newspaper (where her main job was to insert the dollar signs in fruit and vegetable reports). She then relocated to the city, spending eight years at *The Sydney Morning Herald* attracting law suits and generally making a nuisance of herself. During this time, she also conducted a nude interview with American porn star Annie Sprinkle, became a cheerleader for a month and entered the Moscow Circus's infamous Globe of Death on a dare.

Emma now writes a weekly humour column in *The Weekend Australian* where her specialties include subjects as diverse as female fungal disorders, the word 'dipolar' and Belgian porn star Lolo Ferrari's international travel-restricting breast augmentations. She has also written for numerous women's and motorcycling magazines as well as appearing briefly as a men's sex advice columnist in *Max*.

In 1997, Miss Tom won the Henry Lawson Award for Journalism which was awarded for a story on do-it-yourself funerals. Her fiction has appeared in *Dick For A Day*, *Smashed—Australian Drinking Stories* and *Screwed—Stories About Love and Sex*, while her first novel, *Deadset* (a slapstick crime story narrated by a dead schoolgirl) won the Best First Novel section of the prestigious 1998 Commonwealth Writers' Prize for Asia and the South Pacific.

MY ONE TRUE LOVE

Contessa Tom, who is currently working on a second novel with the assistance of an Australia Council grant, recently published a send-up of women's magazines called *Babewatch* with Hodder Headline.

In her spare time she tries not to stack her low-powered motorbike, obtains foolish new tattoos and worries about her hair. Her one true love is her husband Mr David Liam McCormack freelance millionaire, adventure balloonist and lead singer of sleepy death metal band, Custard.

AMY WITTING

A love object can be truly an object, one of the inanimate things of which Auden speaks, that is, if one belongs to the bower bird species as I do.

There is a brooch a reader made for me in his workshop, the head of a girl, the ruffle along her bare shoulder spelling 'A M Y' in delicate lettering. I would not exchange that for an emerald of the same size.

There is a pendant with the miniature glass figure of Kuan Yin, the Goddess of Mercy. That was the gift of a charismatic Chinese lady I met on a plane to Hong Kong.

'Excuse me,' said the youth next to me, 'my aunt is wishing to know, how old are you?'

Ouch! I offered the disagreeable total for translation.

The little woman on his right leaned forward smiling, while her fingers flashed out the same figure.

Nods and smiles.

'Excuse me. My aunt is wishing to know, are you Christian?'

'No. Sometimes I think if Christ was alive now, he would not be Christian either.'

Perhaps that is why she sent me Kuan Yin. At the time, she cured my sinus headache with massage and White Flower embrocation, took the knitted cap off her head and put it on mine, all without dialogue but with obvious goodwill.

Kuan Yin was a good choice. I am comfortable with minor dieties.

I cannot say that my path has been strewn with such offerings, but there are others, tokens of affection, fellowship, immediate affinity, sometimes a wordless thank you from a student, all much cherished.

There are, of course, more serious relationships in my life, but when I read the message of my bower bird collection, I see that my one true love is love itself, in whatever form and wherever I chance upon it.